Spiritual as F*ck

By: Willie Katinowsky

Published by:

Crave Press

www.cravepress.com

Contents

Preface

Hi all,

First and foremost, thank you for picking up this book. More than a title appropriate for the current times, I hope you find this book to be funny, insightful, and ultimately a catalyst for the next step in your journey.

I originally wrote this book over three years before its publication, which is why I wanted to add a quick note to the reader. When I wrote this, I was in a very early stage of my spiritual awakening. Many things were happening and falling into place around me, but at that time, I was still employed by people that were no longer serving my higher purpose. I want to add this note on the front end, as you'll come across several anecdotes about these situations, with no mention of me moving on to greener pastures.

I describe my writing process briefly in this book, but a fair amount of the content, or at least the direction of this content, came from meditating and channeling. I knew at the time that when I finished the book, things would change (and they did), but I had to finish this first. Within a year of finishing this book, I had a new gig, was able to teach yoga and meditation, and have honestly been the happiest I've been since I found my dad's hidden VHS porn stash when I was 11 years old.

I thought about re-writing a lot of these chapters to kind of update things since originally finishing this book, but eventually I realized it wasn't the best course of action. This book came to me as it did, when it did, and there's a reason for that. I don't know what the reason is, but it's the same reason the book is getting published now rather than three years ago, like my former self had hoped for.

They say it's about the journey and not the destination which would be super fucking frustrating to hear if you were running late and your Google maps stopped working as you were navigating the streets of a foreign city; but most likely you are not in that situation as you read this. So, thank you for being a part of my journey and allowing me to be a part of yours.

Sat Nam,

Willie

Introduction

A few years ago, I hit the proverbial rock bottom and realized that I needed to incorporate some type of spirituality into my life. I didn't really know what that would entail, but I knew that if I went on thinking my existence was just some unlucky act of randomness, I was going to end up offing myself sooner or later. Since I knew I didn't have the courage to kick the stool, I instead set forth on my own journey into the realm of spirituality.

As a non-believer, I, of course, had a hard time buying in to some of this hocus pocus, but I didn't feel like I had much of a choice. Books were my main go-to in the beginning of my journey, but at the end of the day, I always felt like the authors were too spiritual to be relatable. I would think things like, "Great for you Deepak, but you've never given a hand-job for crack money, so how does this relate to me?"

Ok, so maybe things never got that bad for me; but if they did, would that mean I could never become "spiritual"? It was this notion that lead me to believe there needed to be a book about spirituality that was a bit more relatable. Where certain religious texts will tell you that you're going to hell if you're "bad," this book says, "Creating hell seems like kind of a dick move in the first place." That's the type of book I was looking for in my journey, so that's the type of book I've written.

So, why am I laying all of this out? Mostly because, when I'm reading, I often find myself trying to figure out the author's intention. Since it's important to me that I create something that I would enjoy as a reader, I think it will be helpful (for both the reader and the writer) to lay out my intentions from the jump.

Like most writers, I am driven by a desire to help others. I am not implying that everyone needs my help, as I know that's not the case, but rather that I want to help whomever I can help. To be more specific, I want to help people become comfortable being honest — honest with themselves, truly authentic. So, goal one is to create honesty by dispelling the fears surrounding it, specifically the fear that others would view us differently if they knew our truths. It is my belief that once that happens, it allows one to realize how truly great they are. Unfortunately, and this says a lot about me, the only way I was able to overcome these fears myself was by realizing how fucked up everyone else is as well. I needed to understand that it wasn't just me, just my family, just my job; it's everyone. Once I realized that every single person I have ever met is as much of a shit show as I am, life became much more manageable. Sure, everyone's fucked-upness is unique to that individual, but my point is, it's there.

It's there in everyone, yet no one really wants to talk about it. Well, I do. And as I opened up and started having these conversations with my friends, I realized how helpful it was to all involved. Soon, I started trying this out with strangers in airports, on planes, at coffee shops, etc. Plane rides were a bit of gamble seeing as if things go south, you're stuck next to that person for the duration of the flight. But you know what? Those conversations never did go south. And why? I don't know for sure, but I'm guessing it's because everyone could benefit from unloading some of the insecurities that are weighing them down. And when finally given the chance to be honest about our thoughts and feelings, we find it refreshing.

If we don't talk about the things that make us insecure, then the only system we have to show ourselves that we are "ok" is through judging others. That may seem helpful in the moment, but it's actually the opposite. When we say things like, "Well at least I'm a better mom than Linda," all we really do is affirm that we are not confident in our own mothering choices, and we create a subconscious guilt for thinking something so terrible about Linda. Ironically, whatever you see in Linda that prompts you to label her a "bad mom" is very likely an observation of a trait or habit that you also exhibit and are self-conscious about. I invite you to take a moment to think about a recent judgement you made about a friend or coworker. Think about it and be honest with yourself. Now, try to trace whatever the judging factor was to your own behaviors or a past situation. Chances are you've done something similar

6

and felt bad about it because it wasn't an awesome thing to do. Whatever your situation was, you don't choose to define yourself by it; so, it would not be wise not to label others accordingly.

Instead of judging others or yourself, just give it away. I'm not suggesting that tomorrow you walk into your employer's office and start bragging about your out of control meth habit, though I do think you'd benefit from telling someone about it if that example applies to you. I am suggesting that you open up. Talk to your friends about your deepest, darkest shit. If you are afraid that they'll judge you, see above. If they are good friends, you will be amazed at what they will offer up in return. You will also end up developing much stronger and authentic relationships.

My second goal in writing this book is to create a conversation about spirituality. This is actually my main goal, but I believe that honesty and spirituality are one and the same. We need to be honest with ourselves about how fucked up we are in order to be ok with it. Once we're ok with it, we invite growth, which is the ultimate form of spirituality.

At this point you may be saying to yourself, "Did this dude really just go from fucked-upness to spirituality?"

Then you might also say, "Well, I guess I can identify as someone who has fucked upness, right?"

Self: "Yeah, but connecting fucked-upness to spirituality? I think this guy might be an asshole."

Also Self: "He's definitely an asshole, but what if our fucked-upness was part of our spirituality?"

Self: "I guess if fucked-upness is a part of me, and being spiritual is a part of me, then they are connected."

Also Self: "I kind of like how this asshole thinks. If being fucked up can make us spiritual, then we are spiritual as fuck."

If that's you, please take a moment to review my statements on judgement, and then relax in knowing that I had that same reaction as I typed the words you just read. Also, stop calling me an asshole. Also, who is the self that we can always converse with? Moving back to fucked-upness and spirituality, these are two seemingly different

7

topics (the first may not yet be recognized as a bona fide topic), but what I noticed about these conversations in fucked-upness is that they always seemed to transition into conversations about spirituality.

At first, I didn't understand why this kept happening, but the more aware of it I became, the clearer the answer became. It circled back to honesty. More importantly, it circled back to the fear of being judged that inhibits honesty. Becoming aware of the prevalence of this fear was one of the gloomiest realizations that I have ever made, second only to the day I realized that pro-wrestling was fake and that my parents were terrible people who encouraged me to believe a lie and were no longer to be trusted.

Seriously though, it is downright depressing to think that so many people are walking around with their anxieties, insecurities, and tough questions about life simply because they are afraid to talk about them. If you believe this doesn't apply to you, then it doesn't. But our egos often encourage us to believe things about ourselves that aren't necessarily true. Our minds are complex and our egos are masters when it comes to self-deceit. No matter how forthright you may be, chances are you are holding back. I used to think I was very forthcoming because I wasn't afraid to say things that others were. Sadly enough, that only confirms the fact that I can be a certified egomaniac. My reality is that I was only saying what I was comfortable telling others. I was creating the illusion of transparency by revealing things that others would not, but keeping the truly vulnerable thoughts to myself. And I was hiding the fact that I was so sickeningly insecure that I often fantasized about no longer having to exist (existential crisis AF).

Maybe it's the fear of being wrong, or the fear of sounding crazy, or just simply the fear of admitting that we don't really have a goddamned clue as to what's going on with our existence. The bottom line is that there is fear there, and that's not helpful. What is helpful is creating a dialog. Let's create meaningful and judgement free conversations about the stuff we are afraid to talk about.

8

The truth is that no matter how different someone may be, we all have one thing in common: we all suffer from the human condition. Part of that malady is wanting to find answers to the big questions. During my own search for these answers, I actually found some. I have been fortunate enough to have some seemingly inexplicable and profound experiences that I now view as spiritual interventions of sorts. But at the time, I was not fortunate enough to have a healthy outlet to process them. Instead, I did what I knew how to do best — I repressed the experiences and went on a vicious campaign to discredit myself in my own psyche. It got so bad that I finally came clean to one of my best friends (true story: we met on the bus ride to kindergarten on the first day of school and are still close to this day). He's a licensed physician, so I was hoping he could diagnose me with lunacy and help me start the process of being committed to a sanitarium. Instead we were able to talk about what I was experiencing and my sanity as two different issues, which they were. I'm not saying he believed everything, but I am saying that it doesn't matter. The point is that the conversation is more important than the fear to have it.

If you were led to read this book, chances are you have already begun to resonate with some of what I have laid out. If not, you're still reading now so there's got to be something that kept you going, right? In any case, as we proceed I am going to try to outline my spiritual journey and then compile a lot of the information that I've learned along the way into something that is honest and easy to understand. At the simplest level, my goal is to write the book that I've been looking for during my own journey.

So, there it is. Now we are both clear on my intentions for writing this, and we can move forward. I like to picture us hand in hand skipping down the proverbial road to enlightenment. But skipping is a lot of work, so we're on Segways instead. Damn, that sounds badass!

Part One

Prophet

When coming up with a title for this book, I originally thought I should ironically refer to myself as a millennial prophet. Watching peoples' faces cringe when I said this out loud led me to believe that it wasn't a great idea, though it definitely got me thinking. I realized that the word itself evokes a seriously heavy reaction from most people, which led me to make it a talking (writing) point.

I am not a prophet. Not in the traditional sense, anyway. And by traditional sense, I mean what I thought a prophet was. I'm not even sure if I'm a millennial, but I assume I am because of the impressive collection of participation trophies that I've acquired over the years. Let me take a moment here to clarify something to my elders: 'twas not we who asked to be given, or came up with the concept of, participation trophies. If not for our elders, we wouldn't even have such a construct to divert attention from the socioeconomic changes throughout the years that are the actual cause of dissonance and misunderstanding between our (and for that matter, all) generations. Possibly more on that later, but back to the prophet thing.

It's quite a ballsy move to refer to oneself as a prophet. It's probably also irresponsible to tie that self-appointed title into a book that you're trying to publish. After simply reading said title, it would be natural to assume that this author lacked a sense of humility, but I can assure you that's not the case here. In fact, I have great humility. The best humility. People are always saying how I'm known for my humility.

Sarcasm aside, the idea of referring to myself as a millennial prophet wasn't originally my idea. If I'm being honest, I don't really feel like writing this book was essentially "my" idea. So whose idea was it, you ask? I'm not entirely sure yet. The thought of writing this book was given to me during an attempt I made to channel my spirit guides while meditating on a plane. For skeptics, now would be an appropriate time to roll your eyes and mutter something to yourself like, "Here we fucking go." I make that point because not too long ago, that would've been my reaction to reading that sentence.

But a lot has changed for me, and not only do I believe in channeling, but I also practice it. For those unfamiliar with channeling, it is essentially a process of communicating with spirit guides/other dimensional beings/ghosts and shit (depending on what you believe). If you don't believe in any of that stuff, then just think of it as a way of communicating with one's subconscious. The truth is, when I'm channeling, I don't know exactly what I'm communicating with, only that the answers I receive are much different than what I would come up with through my own cognitive deductions.

Here's an abridged version of how it went down for me. I had been feeling very lost lately, and though nothing in my life was that bad, I could not seem to maintain any sense of contentment. Though there is rarely one definitive cause for how we feel, I believe that at that time, I really felt that I wasn't working towards any helpful purpose. So in my channeling, I asked for some guidance.

If you're familiar with channeling or communicating with your guides/spirits/the great beyond, then you're already familiar with how this works. For those who are not yet familiar, I want to try to give you an idea of what this is like. Essentially, it is much like a conversation with another person, but without words. Instead, you kind of skip the words step and jump to the understanding. Unfortunately, since we are sufferers of the human condition, we usually need to then convert that understanding into words so that our non-etheric selves can use the information. This works differently for everyone, but I typically preface these conversations with a relaxation meditation and a prayer of gratitude.

So after getting that shit out of the way, here's kind of how this conversation played out:

Me: "Where do I fit in to all this (existence and the unknown realm of spirituality)?"

Ghosts and Shit (G&S): "C'mon, bro, we've been through this like a million times. You already know."

Me: "Right, but what do I *do* with that knowledge?"

G&S: "Help others find their own sense of spirituality using the talents you were given."

Me: "But how?"

G&S: "Be yourself. Be genuine. Tell your story and what you've learned so far."

Me: "Tell who? And how?"

G&S: "The 'who' can't matter to you. The 'how' — write a book."

Me: "Lol, no for real though, how?"

G&S: ...

Me: "I can't write a book. I especially shouldn't write a book about spirituality. You were there, don't you remember all that crazy shit we did back in college and throughout our 20s? I'm a regular guy who's an outlier in bad decision making. Last week, I flipped off an old lady for letting me cut her off. Not too long ago, I didn't even believe in this hocus pocus tomfoolery. That's the reason I'm not the person who should be writing this book."

G&S: "That's exactly the reason why you'd love to write this book."

Me: "Even if I did, what would I call it? *Spiritual AF?*"

G&S: "That makes you sound like a millennial prophet."

Me: "Lol."

I came out of my trance to the sound of me laughing. I really appreciated the sense of humor that was honored during this exchange. Remember, the conversation didn't occur with words, so this re-enactment is merely my way of explaining the feelings and knowledge that was exchanged. But all in all, that is how it went down, and I had a really hard time believing that I could write a book, especially one about spirituality. Maybe I could write a screenplay adaptation, mostly full of dick jokes, that was a Steinbeck parody titled *The Grapes of Shafts,* but certainly not a book on spirituality. (For purchasing information for the rights to *The Grapes of Shafts*, see contact information at the end of this book.)

As unsure as I was, there was also a part of me that profoundly resonated with this idea. Not so much the name, but the concept. Especially earlier on in my journey, I would've cherished a book about spirituality that honestly addressed how bat-shit crazy some of it seemed from traditionally conventional viewpoints. I would've loved to read about the conflicting psyche of a person who recognizes this information as bat-shit crazy while, at the same time, feeling like it's true and they've known it was all along. That's the book I'm writing now. With channeling, the general thought is that you typically get the information that you need at that time. I take that to mean writing this is not my life's purpose, but simply an action that would help me in my ultimate quest to help myself through helping others. I wasn't sure if this would ever get published or if it was a form of therapy my spirit needed. I'm not sure because that's not how this stuff works, and if I waited until I was sure, I'd have never started writing in the first place. But I am sure about the answers that I received that day.

Since writing this, I've received many more answers to many more questions. Not just through channeling, but through genuine life experience as well. Never clear cut and rarely the answers that I think I'm looking for, but answers nonetheless. The questions I have posed are, in essence, the same questions that everyone has. Perpetually unanswerable questions that are part of an ongoing, possibly infinite, conversation. But I was asking where I fit in to all of this, "this" meaning "existence."

From previous journeys within, and simply by analyzing my history, I have already been made aware of two specific things. The first is that I need to help others. It is simply a part of my being that has always existed and always will. It is my most efficient route to personal growth. At times it has allowed me to become a symbolical doormat for some, and at other times it has propelled my ego into a state of laughable self-righteousness. But either way, it has always been there. The less obvious realization was that I have a natural ability to relate to others, and a big part of that is an ability to reframe and redistribute information to promote understanding. I also seem to possess an aptitude for turning any conversation that I'm a part of into a dick joke, but that doesn't hold a lot of relevance at this time.

16

So, here we are. I felt it necessary to shed some light on why I am writing this book and why I felt qualified. More importantly, I wanted to mention why I don't feel qualified. That's the honest truth, so it needs to be part of the conversation. I typically shy away from trying to justify my behavior because it paints the picture that I'm unworthy. It's the whole, "If I don't believe me, why should you?" ordeal. But authoring a book? There's just too much insecurity there, so it needs to be included.

The truth is, the more I opened up, the more right this felt. I love this genre of books, and I am always looking for more books to read within the realm of growth and spirituality. But I found myself always wanting to know more about these people before they became aware. I don't want to read about some spiritual guru who has devoted their life to the service of others. I want to read about a 14-year-old Mother Theresa fat shaming a neighborhood girl because she was jealous of her clothes. Perhaps that never happened, but if it did, wouldn't it make Mother Theresa much more relatable? (Fun fact: In researching examples to use there, I learned that there is a lot of controversy surrounding Mother Theresa and that many think her actions demonstrated her to be a racist homophobe. I'm not sure if that makes referencing her a bad idea or the best idea, but it's there, so deal with it.)

Though I love the books in this realm, from my perspective, the majority of authors seemed a bit too qualified. Yes, I'm judging, and yes, that judgement is only a reflection of my insecurities about not being qualified. Moving on, when I read all this wisdom from these great authors like Deepak Chopra, Elizabeth Gilbert, or Ryan Holiday, I catch myself saying, "Remember, this can't apply to you. These people are great successes. They aren't you."

That view was not serving me. It was unnecessary and ridiculous. What was more ridiculous was the false idea that I held in thinking that the authors I had admired so much didn't have to overcome those same self-harming thoughts. And that brings us back to my motivation for writing this, which will be a re-occurring theme throughout. I want to help others realize for them what I've learned about myself. I want to help people break out of their patterns of self-harming thoughts and behaviors. I want to help people discover their true selves and, what's more, how to love that true-self. I want everyone to have a taste of the serenity that I have found through my journey of spiritual discovery. I don't want to give you my serenity; that's not possible. What I can do is, with good intention, share my experiences as openly and honestly as possible. The rest is out of my hands.

So back to the prophet thing. The simple definition of a prophet is an inspired teacher. And in one way or another, at some point or another, everyone teaches someone else something. It may not be cut and dry, but it's the truth. Yes, I am taking it to that corny place where I say that everyone is a prophet in their own way because your existence is divine in itself, and by simply existing, you help the people you interact with. You help them learn and grow. That means, you are a prophet! Look at you go, you little prophet, you!

We all learn from our interactions because it's in our nature, and we all interact because it's an undeniable part of our existence. Whether we choose to realize that we are inspired or not doesn't really matter. Life becomes a bit easier and a bit more manageable after that realization, but it isn't necessary. You do not need to be aware that you are inspired in order to be inspired, you just simply need to be.

God

Some definitions of "prophet" make specific mention to people who are speaking directly to and even for God. With so many different ideas of who or what God is, definitions tend to become a bit too subjective. The convenience of using the definition of "inspired teacher" is that if one truly believes in God, where else could true inspiration come from except from God? Have you ever had wisdom come to you from an unexpected source? Maybe wisdom came from the person bagging your groceries, an Uber driver, or your four-year-old niece. Perhaps it came from a sentence in an otherwise seemingly shitty book by an author who keeps bringing up his own insecurities.

Regardless of the source, the wisdom was something that you didn't realize you needed to hear, but once heard, it profoundly changed the way you look at things. I have come to believe that it is in those moments that "God" recruits those around us to become prophets. This is why I believe that everyone, even those who don't believe (perhaps them more than others), in their own beautiful and unique way.

What a crock of shit, am I right? That's what I would've thought if I read anything similar a few years ago, though from where I am sitting today (currently the middle seat on flight from Phoenix to Philadelphia, but I'm using "sitting" metaphorically), I can admit that there was also a part of me that identified with those vaguely prophetic statements. They seemed too easy, almost lazy. But yet, they would evoke a reaction in me where I felt obligated to campaign against them, either out loud or as part of that perpetual conversation that occurs in our heads. Had I truly believed them to be false, why would I feel the need to do this? Who was I convincing? I guess the best answer is me? Maybe God? Both? If God is supposed to be in all of us, is there a difference?

God is a touchy subject for most, and rightfully so. To discuss God is to discuss the very nature and purpose of one's existence, which is why people tend to get exceedingly defensive when their concept of God is challenged. Protective defense mechanisms coupled with the unending variety of beliefs of what God actually is make it a nearly impossible subject to discuss cordially.

People need a purpose, some type of meaning. Without some goal or focus or feeling of belonging, it won't take long for even the brightest of people to slowly wither out of existence (existence in the human form, that is). As people, we long to be part of something much bigger and better than ourselves. It helps formulate that purpose if we believe we are here for a reason. Religion, though great for some, can, for others, prey on this very human desire. Rather than search for our own answers to the unanswerable questions, religions provide a nice and convenient checklist to be followed. If life were truly a test, then religion would be the answer key. Whether right or wrong, religion is the backbone upon which many build their sense of purpose and their sense of identity. This is why most become defensive when their ideas are challenged. This is also why groups of people are able to repeatedly do horrible things in the name of their God. These terrible acts aren't done because these people are so confident in their beliefs; it's the complete opposite.

History is full of powerful people wiping out civilizations of less powerful people in the name of God. Wherever you are right now, in whatever country, at some point in its formation, God and religion played a major role. But that's in the past, so let's look at a more recent example — the "God hates fags" people (their organization will not be getting a shout-out in this book, so I will only be referring to them as that). Seriously, no person who was actually secure in their belief system would find it necessary to go to a craft store (I imagine JOANN or Michael's), buy the supplies, use a chosen artistic medium to create a sign that says "God Hates Fags," and then hold said sign out in public. Try as I might to not judge, I can't help but laugh when I picture these people shopping for supplies and picking just the right color for their artwork.

It all seems so silly to me, but I digress. If those people really felt that was the truth, they would not need to validate their beliefs by holding demonstrations. The only type of person who would do that was someone seeking to cope with the fact that they really have no idea what's going on. Such an act would be a confession that they are cripplingly insecure in their beliefs and that they are terrified. So, any time you see a sign saying that God hates fags, imagine it displaying what it is really saying: "I Am Scared."

Now, I don't want it to seem like I'm picking on the God hates fags people. I'm not a bully. My reaction to them used to be very similar to what they tend to promote — anger and hate — until I was able to see them for what they are. They are terrified just like everybody else. I was so angry that I loved to use their actions to justify my argument to others that God didn't exist. If God existed, why would he allow them to do that in his name? There were many things that I questioned — children with cancer, anyone with cancer, 9/11, all bad shit in general. God couldn't exist if all of that stuff happens, right? It took me a while, but I realized that God wasn't the problem; I was the problem.

So, how did a devout atheist get to writing a book about spirituality? Here's the synopsis. I was raised to be Catholic and, surprisingly, that didn't end up working out. My family was actually Polish Catholic which I swear is a thing (go ahead and ask Siri, I'll wait). It's very similar to Roman Catholic except our church's submarines had screen doors. (If you don't get that joke, call your oldest living, and socially accepted racist, relative and ask them to explain "the good old days.) Ok, so maybe I don't remember what the differences were, but it doesn't really matter. What did matter for me was that I just wasn't buying it. And I don't know if it was just part of growing up, but I really didn't want to believe it.

I remember that during confirmation class, they taught us that once we were confirmed, we were to be held responsible for our sins in the eyes of God and the church henceforth. The only other thing I remember learning was that the only unforgivable sin was not believing in God. Rape and murder were cool if you went to confession, but if you did not believe, you were done forever. That was pretty much it for me in terms of religion. To seal that deal, I made

21

sure that the very night after getting confirmed, I prayed to God so I could tell "him" that I didn't believe.

I didn't really have a firm grasp on irony at that time so I wasn't able to see how absurd that action was, but once the prayer was said, I was instantly overcome with fear and possibly guilt. I was 12 years old, so I didn't dwell on it for too long as I had recently discovered boobs and they were much more fun to dwell on. I don't remember exactly what I did immediately after saying what would be my last prayer for almost two decades, but knowing me I probably put on the blurred in Spice channel and drifted off into a carefree slumber. By the time I was 16 years old, I was able to use the actions of other churchgoers to convince my parents that I didn't need to go to church at all. I also got much better at the internet, so I didn't need the spice channel either. Talk about growth!

I spent the next 15 years telling others, but really trying to convince myself, that I was an atheist. And like many people who are deeply insecure in their beliefs, I was a bit of a dick about it. But that's how it works. When you're unsure about something, believing you're better than those who think differently is your ego's way of helping you cope with the fact that you're just being an asshole.

Sometime after I turned 30, an acquaintance of mine dropped some unexpected prophetic wisdom on me while sharing a bit about his own journey. Amidst the bedlam of details in which I wasn't particularly interested, Michael made the following confession: "It's not that I didn't want to believe in God, but I didn't want to be the type of person that believed in God." That was a game changer for me. It's always an incredible experience when someone that you don't really know can call you out on your shit without even intending to.

Hearing Michael's revelation was humbling and also one of my first clear looks into the true power our egos can have if we let them. It also helped me remember that it is ok to believe in an unknown higher power. Previously, my ego would tell me that such beliefs would make me stupid or weak. I thought that God was for people who were too unstable to deal with the realities of life, so they'd cling to fairytales. The truth is that I am about as unstable as they come, and I was the one who was clinging to a false reality.

Now I'm not saying that my church was right about God. I am saying, however, that my church wasn't right for me. The truth is that it's never the truly devout followers who condemn other religions. Those with real connections to their God tend to shy away from condemning in general. In fact, the same priest whom I disagreed with during confirmation also preached how important it was to be accepting of other beliefs and even borrowed teachings from other religions from time to time. Reflecting on his wisdom, I came to believe that maybe the act of believing was more important than the belief itself.

By realizing that religion was not a prerequisite for faith, I decided that perhaps I was ready to give God another shot. And by simply allowing myself to believe that there could be a higher power behind all of this, I began to see evidence of God's existence all around. In fact, where I used to view science as a vehicle to disprove God's existence, I now understand that science has done the exact opposite.

My personal favorite example of this is our body. When you break it down, it's simply a fucking miracle. We have trillions of cells that can self-replicate, delegate responsibility, and actually change and adapt to our needs. The sheer quantity of "trillions" is enough for me to believe in a God since I have a hard time simply conceiving that amount. For my own comprehension, I need to dumb that down to "a lot." But then as you go deeper and examine the different types of cells in our body, the different systems, it's incredible. To think that this has all come about by series of random occurrences and genetic mutations is a bigger leap of faith than believing in some type of God.

Now, I'm not implying that evolution isn't the cause of our current physical state, because I personally believe that it is. I am instead posing the question, what is the cause of evolution? Personally, evolution, which used to be my "proof" that God doesn't exist, is now "proof" to me of God's existence. For those who still maintain that it was the result of random events, I don't disagree there either. But I probably have a different idea of what random is. Maybe random is just another name for God.

This brings us back to an interesting question: What is God? Please understand that in no way whatsoever am I trying to answer that question for anyone else. I couldn't if I wanted to. I maintain that I do not know what God is, and I accept that I will never have a complete answer to such a question.

Where I'm at right now, I view God as an energy that connects all of us with everything in the entire universe. God, to me, is everything that has ever existed and everything that has not. More still, my definition of God seems to be ever changing and growing as my journey continues. And I like it that way. That works for me. I think it is imperative that everyone stick with what works for them. Who knows what my idea of God will be years from now. Maybe I'll relapse on atheism, or maybe I'll become a Hind-Jew (Hindu and Jewish combo), or perhaps one day I'll be standing on your doorstep manically explaining that I have recently realized that *you* are God! I don't know what the future holds but I know that focusing on what could be distracts from what is. And what my God right is now is my journey.

I truly believe that the actions of pursuing a spiritual journey are more important than the knowledge gained. If we rely on the knowledge alone, our journey stops once knowledge is obtained, and we have no choice but to cling to our belief. When the journey is our focus, we constantly build upon our knowledge, thus enhancing our experience. Sure, our beliefs may change throughout the journey, but we will always be able to replace dispelled beliefs with a new course of direction, leading eventually to new beliefs that are a better fit for who we are at that time.

The only way someone can pursue an authentic journey is by being true to themselves, and that starts with tuning in to what feels right to you. That feeling of rightness, or resonance which we will discuss later, is our compass and will always steer us in the direction we need to go. From my experience, that direction seldom makes sense at that time, but it doesn't need to. The direction isn't important; all that matters in your journey is that you set sail.

Awakening Part 1: Awakening to My Awakening

Here's what happened when I set sail. My first conscious experience with something "otherworldly" came to me in a kundalini yoga class in Huntington Beach, California. I must classify it as conscious because it was the first time I was aware of what I was experiencing. I am certain that we all participate in ethereal events every day, but we've conditioned ourselves to discount them. Children, being newer to existence in this form and having experienced less societal conditioning, are said to be more in touch with the spirit realm. It is less likely that this occurs because of age and much more likely that, as children, they have not yet developed the defense mechanism of skepticism, though like everything this is probably the result of a combination of many factors.

Back to yoga. So, I had been practicing kundalini yoga for a few months and never had anything apparently life-changing happen. Kundalini yoga is a very specific type of yoga that originated in India and focuses on fostering the awakening of one's kundalini energy (now would be a great time to Google some shit). I didn't know that when I started attending classes; all I knew about it was that they had a very affordable Groupon. Class was certainly not what I expected and involved a lot of chanting, meditating, and, eventually, gongs. The instructor was also dressed in all white garb and went by a spiritual name of her choosing in lieu of her government name. Street gang members also commonly choose to identify with a chosen moniker to demonstrate devotion, so the concept was not entirely new to me.

I quickly learned that these classes were not what I thought yoga was going to be, and they often involved weird breath patterns coupled with chanting in a foreign language. As someone who was completely unaware of the practices of this community, my initial reaction was what most would consider typical: "This shit is bananas." Lucky for me, life had humbled me enough by this point that I knew hanging around certainly couldn't make any aspect of my life worse, so I stuck it out through the duration of the Groupon. Had I walked into a run of the mill vinyasa/hatha studio, my yoga habit probably would not have lasted; but fortunately for me, that wasn't the case.

The more I attended class, the more I felt drawn to this place. It just felt right. Sometime around my third month, we were sitting in easy pose (not actually easy for me) and practicing some intense breathwork when I felt it. I can't tell you exactly what "it" was, but it was definitely something. The best way I can describe what I experienced was a small ball of energy in my lower torso that was moving in a figure eight pattern. A quick WebMD search told me it was definitely cancer (which is the result of every WebMD search ever), but I had a hunch that it might be something else. The movement of this energy was very subtle and created a slight rocking motion in my body. I have since learned that this was the beginning of my kundalini awakening. (Kundalini awakening is a cooler and more dramatic way of saying the activation of my kundalini energy.)

Like any rational human being, I clung on to my skepticism throughout this experience. I even hoped to find a debunking explanation on the internet. Maybe this was a random firing of core muscle fibers, firing in a sequence that created this rocking or something to that affect. But I couldn't find that explanation anywhere. I had also spent a large portion of my life as an athlete and have developed an above average sense of body awareness. I know what cramps, spasms, and any uncontrolled muscles firing feels like, and this wasn't that. This wasn't anything that I had previously experienced, and it wasn't anything that I could explain.

Now I know this doesn't sound like much, and in a way, it really isn't. But given the context of what this meant to me in terms of my spiritual journey, it was monumental. This was my first conscious experience receiving affirmation that there is something else going on in my existence. I didn't know what it was, just that it was. In the end, that's all I needed. I needed a little push, not in any specific direction, just something to tell me to start paying attention.

After that day, I started cultivating more similar experiences. Maybe I had cultivated them in the past, but I was now consciously aware of these experiences. Some were in class as a result of meditations, and some were more awesome coincidences that kept putting me where I needed to be.

Ask anyone who has had a legit awakening of their own, and they will tell you a similar tale. Once I became open and aware to whatever was happening, it was nonstop. The more I searched for answers, the more questions I received. But that was ok with me because for the first time ever, I felt like I was truly in communication with the universe, with God.

At that time, I still hadn't fully trusted the universe to provide for me despite my numerous inexplicable experiences, so I cultivated more. But that wasn't enough. I wanted more God. If I could have tied off and shot God into my veins, I would have. But that's weird, and I couldn't, so I found books and podcasts to help get information. I didn't know exactly what information I was looking for so, via the suggestion of my yoga teacher, I would just ask for "the right" information to come to me and somehow it would.

To give a quick example of how this works, when I was in a bit of a funk and felt very stagnant, I decided that I was going to get a new book that was going to open my eyes to some new spiritual topics. So, I set that intention and I prayed and meditated about it. I decided that this would happen on a trip to my favorite second hand book store. Once I got in there, I would open myself up and be led to the book I needed. This was going to be a great experience, and I was going to get some real-time feedback affirming that I'm super good at this God stuff.

Well, when I checked the internet to see what time the bookstore opened, I found out it was closed. Fuck. All of that for nothing. A bit disheartened, I decided I would go about my day, and first up was laundry. As I pulled up to the laundromat, it was empty, which was really odd for a Saturday morning. Seriously, I had been using this laundromat for a few years and that was the only time I'd ever been the only person in it. Anyway, my initial reaction was asking myself if it was closed, which I immediately received an answer within telling me that it was open. More of a "just go in" feeling. The second I stepped foot inside, I saw there was a book on top of the trashcan. No one around. Just a book.

You can probably see where this is going but, I was a little freaked out. It was too convenient. I knew in my being that this book was there for me, but I was afraid to look at it. Like an idiot, I didn't want to pick it up. I guess I was scared that it wouldn't be what I was looking for, like it was probably book 32 of the *Boxcar Children.* Eventually, I gave in and picked it up. It was *Superbeings* by John Randolph Price.

I had no idea who that guy was or what he was about, but that was the exact book I was looking for at that time. The irony there is that if I would've went to the bookstore, I never would've given that book consideration. But that's not what happened. Instead, God or the universe, same thing to me, made an idiot-proof plan for this idiot to read that book.

What was in that book? Well, it was essentially a "how to" guide on tapping into your inner God self to maximize your potential. I can't say that I particularly resonated with it wholeheartedly at that time, but simply reading it helped me put some other ideas that were floating around in my head into perspective. It was another step in the right direction. It wasn't a book I needed to read for the content; it was the book I needed to read to keep growing.

If you are a good skeptic, like I've been known to be, then you probably see that situation as follows: Some bro left a shitty book on a trash can and this bro thinks it was an act of God. I can't refute that. All I can offer is that I see those two instances as the same thing.

I think the biggest takeaway from these examples is recognizing that they are subtle. The yoga, finding the book; these are only two of the numerous inexplicable events I have experienced since the start of this journey. So, if there were other events, why would I focus on these two? It's certainly not because they were fun to read about. I chose these events because they were incredibly uneventful. Either could've been easily overlooked and completely ignored. I'm sure that in the past I have ignored similar happenings. These events taught me the importance of paying attention. The answers will come if you let them, and only if you let them. It's hard to follow directions if you refuse to read the street signs. But once you learn to follow your path, you will allow yourself to be led to much more exciting destinations. You will begin to receive much less subtle signs (for an example of a less subtle sign, please read the next chapter).

Awakening Part 2: My Space Adventure

Spirituality is an abstract concept, making the idea of a spiritual awakening an abstract concept. So, here's the tale of my abstract concept that led to a greater sense of another abstract concept. I don't think a spiritual awakening can be simplified down to one specific event or moment, though it is convenient to do so for the sake of explanation. But if I had to pick a very clear defining experience to label as my awakening, then this is what I would chose.

New to the realm of spirituality and mindful living, I had been practicing yoga steadily for about four months. As I stated in the last chapter, I could feel the positive effects it was having on my life which prompted me to do some research and acquire whatever information was available. And at that time, a lot of information that I was getting seemed to circle back to the chakras. A guest on one of my now favorite podcasts (a podcast that I also unknowingly stumbled upon on my search) even suggested that in order to fully receive from the universe, one must be sure to first open up (the chakras). In essence, you can't put money in your wallet unless you open it first. That made sense to me, so I took some time and developed my own meditation where I spent about an hour total, roughly seven minutes each, focusing on each energy center and asking for them to be open. I didn't feel much different at the time, but I would learn later that I had succeeded in my quest for openness.

A few hours after my experimental chakra ceremony, I began to wind down for bed, though I wasn't tired. I was lying on my couch watching something mindless on Netflix, and I suddenly had an intense urge to turn it off. I can't quite explain it, but I just had to have silence and darkness. Almost like receiving instructions, I felt the need to get in one last meditation in for the day. I didn't think much of it. At the time, I viewed it as my body hinting to me that I needed to try to ready myself for sleep. As I drifted into that special state between wakeful thought and thoughtless sleep, I received a very clear-cut communication from something that was not me. I didn't know what I was communicating with, but I knew distinctly that it was something else. I did not hear distinct words or sentences, but I received thoughts or feelings that I could translate into words. Here's the how the conversation played out:

Something Else (SE): "Do you want this?"

Me: "Yes, of course I want this."

SE: "Are you sure you want this?"

Me: "Hell yeah! Who wouldn't want this?"

I have to admit that during that conversation, I did not know what this was. But I knew I wanted it. At the exact moment that I agreed to receive "this," I felt an intense pulling sensation, like my entire being was at the bottom of a bungee jump at that precise moment when you experience the maximum amount of tension before getting launched back into the air. Then, in a matter of what seemed like a fraction of a second, I was sucked out into the cosmos.

It happened in an instant, though as I experienced it, I distinctly saw myself get pulled away from the earth, then away from our galaxy, and then into some seemingly random place in the universe. In this brief moment, I did not have a body. I did not have eyes but could clearly see the celestial formations around me. I didn't have a brain but was clearly experiencing thoughts and feelings. I wish I had a cooler story so I could tell you all about how I was able to embrace my new form of existence as I explored this realm of limitless possibility. Unfortunately, that is not my story.

The truth is, I was terrified. Now, to be fair, I had never existed without my body before, so I need you to cut me some slack; but I was very aware that I didn't have a body in that moment. This created a problem as a part of me was terrified about what was happening, and I began to think, "I do not want this. I was wrong. I do not want this." Again, I received instant action from my communication and was sucked back down into my body that was on my couch in my now pointless and infinitesimal apartment. Don't say it because I already know — I totally wussed out. But there's more.

Somewhere along my journey back into my body, I felt something join with me, almost guiding me back into my regular existence. The second it attached to me, my insurmountable fear was washed away, and I felt immense comfort. I knew everything was ok and that I was loved. Back in my body, I was unable to move but I could see clearly, more clearly than I could if my eyes were open as I typically need to wear glasses, but I wasn't yet seeing with my physical eyes. Everything in my apartment was exactly the same as it was before my space excursion except for one thing. There was now a tall slender woman sitting on the arm of my Ikea Poäng chair and looking down on me. She was in long, grayish robes and had long, brown hair. Weirder still, I couldn't see her face at the time but I knew exactly what her face looked like. Again, I know some of this sounds odd, but this is the best way I can explain what I experienced. Our vocabularies were not developed to describe the inexplicable. But as she sat there, without speaking, she clearly transmitted much needed information to me. She "told" me that everything was ok and that I was safe; that no matter what, even in death, I will be ok and safe; and lastly that she, and others, will always be with me and always have been. All I could do was send back a very gracious "thank you" and then, at that very moment, I blinked my physical eyes open and she was gone.

Any skeptics who are reading this will rightfully think I am misinterpreting a dream as a spiritual experience. I would've thought the same if I was simply reading this and hadn't experienced it myself. Unfortunately, I don't have any physical evidence to back up my claims. I can only state that I have experienced countless dreams before, and this was not that. What I experienced was incredibly real and incredibly unique to me. In fact, I have been unable to replicate this experience and as a result began to doubt it myself. But then, in typical fashion, the universe sent me a little message to make sure I would not discount what I experienced.

This time the message did not involve space travel or a mysterious ghost woman, but instead a wonderful kundalini yoga instructor named Shuba. Now for the sake of understanding, I need to back track a bit to create a big picture concept here to explain how this came to be. After my trip to space, I had so many questions that I was in a desperate hunt for information. I read or listened to as much as I could, and every night I prayed and asked God or the universe or whatever to guide me to the information that I was seeking. During this time, there was a three day period where Reiki was suggested to me once a day in succession from three different sources.

First, a friend suggested I look for a local training, but that suggestion didn't yet resonate with me. The next day, a book I was reading which had nothing specifically to do with Reiki brought up the subject as a good intro into meditative practices that nourish spiritual experiences. Interesting, but I still didn't feel sold on the idea. The day after that, the guest on a podcast I was listening to mentioned that Reiki was her personal launching point into her spiritual journey. Three days in a row seemed to be more of a sign than a coincidence, so I gave in and started looking for trainings in my area.

Since I felt like the universe was telling me to do this, I assumed that I would find a convenient training in no time, but I was surprised to find nothing of the sort. I searched the internet for a while and found that all the local trainings had either just passed or were months away. I was a bit bummed but, more than anything, I was upset with myself for being dumb enough to believe that the universe was guiding me to do something. Seriously, I didn't even know what Reiki actually was, so how could I be so naive to think I was meant to practice it?

Trying not to be too hard on myself, I went back to life as usual, and that meant yoga class in the morning. Upon arriving at class, there was a woman named Mary whom I had never met before and who promptly introduced herself to me. We talked briefly before class started, and I learned that she was also a yoga instructor at this studio. Then right as the conversation dwindled down and we were about to start class, she handed me a flyer from her bag as she mentioned that she was a reiki master and would be holding a training at her house (only a few miles from my apartment) in two weeks. So, in less than 12 hours, I went from believing that the universe was guiding me, to thinking

I'm a fool for entertaining such beliefs, to being affirmed that the universe was in fact communicating with me directly.

The day of the training, I almost decided to skip it. It's not that I had anything better to do, but that I had again lost faith in my own quest for spirituality. As the author of this book about spirituality, I would love to be able to make it sound as if I was a fearless trailblazer filled with unrelenting faith, but it's important that you know that the reality of this is quite the contrary. That morning in particular, I had completely lost faith in my own experiences. I felt like nothing in my life was changing how I thought it should (poor me), and I had rationalized that my trip to space was in fact a dream. Even more, I told myself that I was an idiot for needing to believe in magic forces in lieu of accepting responsibility for my own shitty life.

But since I had already paid for the training and I did still believe in the idea that I shouldn't waste money, I decided to go. During the morning session, I experienced a few other-worldly physical sensations where I could actually feel this reiki energy. That was pretty cool as it started to restore my faith in the idea that something bigger was at play here (existence). Then at lunch we were all talking about life and the different areas of our life that led to us attending the Reiki training. Then suddenly one of my classmates, Shuba, felt the urge to share about an experience that she had over a decade ago.

It was a bit off topic and may have seemed out of the blue to everyone, but not to me. I think it even caught her off guard because she started her story off by saying, "I'm not sure why, but I'm feeling compelled to share this with you all." Now in the yoga community, people say stuff like that all the time, so I didn't think much of it until she was trying to explain that bungee cord feeling you experience the split second before you get sucked out into space.

I couldn't believe it. She was having a hard time explaining the sensation, and I knew why. It's a fucking hard thing to explain. My bungee cord analogy is ok, I mean it's the best I can come up with, but it doesn't really do it justice. Either way, as she went on with her story, it was the exact same — the sensations we felt, not having a body, giving permission in the beginning. The only difference is that she wasn't terrified. Besides the fact that I am a bit of a coward, I attribute this to the timing of her experience. She was actually at a yoga retreat when this occurred and had been living a spiritual life for over 20 years. My experience occurred a few months after signing up for a yoga Groupon. I think that Shuba was more ready than I.

The point of all of this is that I needed to hear Shuba's story, and I needed to hear it at the right time. Had I heard it before my experience, I most certainly would have discounted it. If I had heard it right after I went to space, it would have been easy for me to lump in with my own experience and discount them together. Had I heard her tale much later, I probably would have already succeeded in convincing myself my own experience was a lie and I doubt I would have listened. One never knows what would actually happen in these hypothetical situations, so I'll focus on what did happen. When I lost faith, I asked for guidance and, most importantly, I remained open to receive it.

Besides receiving affirmation of my own experience, I learned an important lesson about following the path. Asking to be led only works if you're willing to be led. That would be like getting directions from your GPS but deciding you'd rather try to find your own way. You might still get there, but then why would you waste the energy and precious data from your greedy cell phone provider by using your GPS in the first place?

If you're going to ask for guidance, be sure to keep an eye out for the guidance. The messages we receive are subtle and can easily be discounted. It would be fantastic if we could get sucked out into space at will or receive definitive answers immediately upon the posing of our questions, but that's not how things work, and there must be a reason for that. My tale of accidental space travel makes a great story for a spiritual awakening. But the truth is, my awakening happened well before that. By paying attention to the subtleties of my existence, I was led to such an experience, but it had to happen in that order. It's a lot easier to pay attention to the road conditions after your tires hydroplane on a puddle, but if you pay attention to the road from the beginning of your commute, chances are you'll avoid the puddle all together.

<u>Journey</u>

Not long after developing my dependency on God, I took a new approach to my quest for spirituality. My awakening was my Ygritte reminding me that just like John Snow, I know nothing. (If you don't get my Game of Thrones reference, I applaud you in straying from the trends, but you're missing out.) Seriously, before that day, there was no way that I'd believe someone if they told me that they had experienced what I just divulged to you. Even if it was someone I trusted, I would have rationalized some explanation in my head — that they believe what they're saying, they just don't realize their mind was playing a trick on them. I'm certainly not proud of how closed minded I was, but that's just the reality of where I was then, and it's certainly where I would expect many readers to be. In order for me to feel comfortable in my existence, I had to believe that I knew best, no matter what. I believed myself to be the authority on God simply because I was sure he couldn't exist. Pathetic? Yes, but also very human.

Experiencing the all source, God, or whatever you want to call it was innately humbling because it showed me that I simply don't have all the answers (not in the way that I thought). Deep down, I had always known that I didn't have all the answers, but insecurities fed my ego which essentially blinded me from my own truth. Luckily, like all things crafted in falsehood, the facade was eventually broken down and I was humbled back into the truth.

Through humility came freedom when I was finally able to let go of my ego and adapt an entirely new philosophy on all things spiritual (All things in existence? Just all things?). Instead of being skeptical about everything, which I tried to no avail, I decided that I would instead accept everything. I didn't decide to blindly believe everything that was presented to me, but I was able to look at other schools of thought and say to myself, "Who are you to say that's not how it works? Remember, you know nothing."

It was that new approach that has launched me on the amazing journey that you are now a part of in this very

41

moment. Whether this is a published book as I initially intended, a blog, or a Microsoft Word document that showed up in your inbox completely unsolicited, you are now a part of my journey. And even if you've resonated with absolutely nothing I've written or you've hated every word you've read, in some way, I'm now part of your journey as well. That brings us back to why I am writing this (again?).

If this writing encourages just one person to embark on their own spiritual journey, or even just initiates a mind shift where they can entertain the idea of embarking on a spiritual journey, then it was worth the time that I put into it. If this influences absolutely no one to do anything, then it was still worth my time, just not in a way that I have yet to understand.

What I'm learning is that most of the lessons that are delivered to me throughout this journey are delivered in ways I cannot predict and can rarely comprehend initially. I've come to believe that's how this universe works. A series of seemingly innocuous coincidences are strung together and suddenly become what looks like a masterfully laid out plan. A coincidence is only a coincidence until we can figure out how to attach some meaning or purpose to it. Keeping that in mind, I'd like to share some personal examples of how this has worked so far in my own experience.

I've been in a job that I thought I hated for the past 10 years. As a millennial, I was not supposed to stay in my first job this long. We're supposed to make a bunch of lateral moves, each with an increasing salary and new experiences to add our resumes. Well, since I never had a career goal in mind, making moves was never really a priority. I completely stumbled into my job and never left.

Currently (as of writing this, but hopefully not as of you reading this), I work for a non-profit boarding school that gives adjudicated at-risk youth a chance to turn their lives around.

Disclaimer: I want to be clear in stating that I absolutely love my job for the opportunities it has given me to help teenagers turn their lives around. When I say that I'm hopeful I no longer work for them, it's more that I hope I have learned how to become financially independent from my current employer. As trying as the job has been at times, I truly believe in the work the school is doing, and I hope to one day be a benefactor and hopefully a board member for this organization. There will be examples in this book where it sounds like I'm being ungrateful for my job, and that's because I have been ungrateful at times. I don't want my honesty to dissuade from the fact that I am truly grateful for the lessons learned and the opportunities given through this non-profit organization. Ok, back to business.

What I thought was just going to be my first "adult" job ("adult" because it included health insurance) turned out to be the most valuable educational experience I could ever receive. I learned more in my first two years of working there than I did in my entire college career. Admittedly, that may not be saying much as I once attended a class in which I was never enrolled for an entire semester. I'd be lying if I said weed wasn't involved, and I don't lie, so I won't say that. Anyway...

Even though this school that I work for is in Pennsylvania, the area where I spent most of my life, the job gave me the opportunity to live in California which had always been a dream of mine. But that came to be in a way that I couldn't have foreseen.

In 2008, I was hired as a teacher/counselor and quickly became the go-to for my supervisor. I was such a kiss ass that my coworkers nicknamed me the golden boy. I may not have been super popular, but I was a company man for sure even though the work was thankless and the pay was worse. As time passed, I worked my ass off but ended up getting held back from any promotions. The management structure in these places is not good. Despite my inappropriate loyalty to my bosses, they blocked me from any movement that could have made my seemingly shitty circumstances slightly less shitty. At my five-year mark, I got passed up for a promotion that I felt I deserved. I was fucking livid. I could not wrap my head around the decision that was made. Having had enough, I started undermining my bosses at every opportunity that came my way. I'm not super proud of that, but you'll never guess what happened.

I got promoted. Twice in six months. First, I got promoted to the better schedule that I had been asking for the past three years. Then six months later, I got promoted to a position that would move me to California, give me control over my schedule, and come with a housing allowance. That's right, free rent in southern California and I got to make my own schedule. How did this happen?

Well for one, if I would've gotten that promotion that I felt I was owed, I never would've even applied for the California position. So what I thought was the biggest travesty of the century was of course a blessing in disguise. I should add that I didn't originally get the position in California either. It was given to a friend of mine whom I was genuinely happy for. Instead of being a spiteful dick per my usual tendencies, I was truly happy that my friend and fellow Pennsylvania native was going to get to start a new life in California. But then a few weeks later, some decisions were made that two people were going move to California instead of one, and we got to move out here together.

That would be an amazing coincidence if there was such a thing as coincidence. As I've read more and more books on the law of attraction and manifestation, I have come to believe that the universe gave me this opportunity once I was ready. Instead of believing that I would never get promoted or never live in California, I only focused on being happy for my friend. I think it also helped that I wasn't trying to manifest anything at the time either. If I would've been happy for him in an attempt to get something in return, it would not have been genuine, and I believe things would've worked out differently.

But I was genuinely happy for him, and it worked out in an amazingly unforeseen way. It was in California that I gained some valuable life lessons and a plethora of perspective into my own self-limiting behaviors. I have always been a lofty dreamer with "unrealistic" aspirations. I believed that the things I wanted were unrealistic. Let's think about that. Why would anyone go through the trouble of wanting something that was unobtainable? I don't know, I'm fucking insane? Probably, but also, nothing is unobtainable. It took me a while to realize this, but I know it to be a fact now. Initially I had to borrow from the experiences of others, reading any book or article I could about success stories of people who seemingly came from nothing and were able to generate their own success and the life of their dreams.

I love reading those stories. Who doesn't? It's inspiring and can fill the reader with hope. The thought that no matter where you are in life or what has happened, you can turn it around. As much as I wanted to believe that, I could never fully believe in that for myself. I always looked at those stories like, "Yeah she went from battling addiction and wanting to kill herself to becoming the most famous author of the century. But that's her. She's just incredibly special. That could never be me."

Part of that thought is true, she is incredibly special. But so is everyone else. Every person on this planet has a gift, talent, or passion that can uplift others and elevate the frequency of those around them. Not everyone is going to be a famous author, but not everyone wants that. There are people being born right now that are going to invent jobs and careers that don't exist yet. The key to the success for any of these people is the belief system they adopt. The first step for me was switching my own attitude from "That's not me" to "Why not me?" It sounds like simple idea, but it took me over a year of reciting this mantra to actually start believing it. Even now as I am writing this, I go through waves of doubt and self-deprecation, but the positive thoughts occupy more space than the negative. It's basic, but it's a win.

Again, if you're reading this, I totally understand that this could come across like some positive thinking scam: A reading promoted by some pyramid scheme weight-loss tea. Maybe this long-winded entry seems straight from the diary of a psychopath (maybe that's all this is). In any case, I'm still writing and you are apparently still reading, so why stop now?

Realizations

As stated earlier, it is impossible for us to fully understand how this universe works. That's part of the human condition. It's one of the constants throughout each and every human experience. Some may understand more than others, but no one can understand it all; not in human form. Even if we answered some of life's greatest and most mysterious questions, we would find greater and more mysterious questions to have. We want knowledge, and we are greedy. But if we're going to be greedy with something, we could certainly pick things much worse than knowledge.

I have realized in my journey that the way my universe works is that my spirit, my inner being, already contains the knowledge I am looking for. I say *my* universe because I don't want to presume that I know how things work for you. Do I believe this is how things work for you? Yes. Does that matter? No. Well, it shouldn't matter to you. This will only be your truth if you discover it to be so.

The answers are within. This vague proclamation annoys me because for many years, I looked at that statement as a cliché. And it certainly is. But there is nothing more annoying than a cliché that proves itself right. If you don't believe me, all I ask is that you take some time to honestly try to look within for some knowledge. It could be about anything. It could be as simple as posing the question, "Do I have any knowledge within?" Ask and try. Even if the answer is, "No, you don't have knowledge within," that in itself is an answer. And it is knowledge you somehow got from within. Weird, right?

Back to realizations. Today, as I was participating in a gong relaxation and meditation at the end of a kundalini yoga class (new age AF), I had a realization about realizations: By simply using the term "realization," we imply that this is knowledge that we already have. We don't call realizations "lessons learned" because we know there is a difference. A lesson may certainly lead to magnificent realizations, but it's not a prerequisite. A realization is simply the understanding of knowledge that we already have and can occur at the most seemingly unexpected times.

This is what I offer any skeptics out there who may not yet believe there is a metaphorical library of knowledge within. Think about any realization you may have had. It's different from learning a new concept or idea. If I told you that Cap'n Crunch's full name was Captain Horatio Magellan Crunch, and like any good reader you quickly fact checked this on Google, that is information that you have learned. Something you didn't previously know (unless you did, in which case please close this book immediately, tell your cats you'll be back later, and go make some friends), and you read the information and now you do know it.

A realization is different. It's a bit harder to explain (as are all things metaphysical), but it just feels different. It tends to happen out of the blue or in unexpected ways. You suddenly understand something that you previously did not, yet you did that without introducing any external information. So how is that possible? Where was this stored? Scientists and psychotherapists may offer the explanation that it's information that was stored in your subconscious. I like that explanation. But what's a subconscious? What's a conscious? What's a thought? Immediately responding to answers with more questions — that's how my mind works (what's a mind?).

But seriously, science can only explain so much. Thoughts are said to be a series of electrical impulses and chemical reactions that occur in the brain. I went through most of my life so far accepting that as an answer. But what does that "answer" even mean? How do electricity and chemical reactions yield our experiences and perceptions? I'm not implying that they don't. I'm simply pointing out that by themselves, those two forces are the scientific explanation for you seeing everything you've ever seen, hearing everything you've ever heard, etc. Is it not possible that there is more going on? Is it not possible that science is limited by only being able to use what it has proven thus far when offering explanations?

There were times in history where electricity wasn't a concept, nor was the idea of chemical reactions, yet people still had thoughts. There were times in history where people thought Earth was the center of the universe. That was scientific fact then. Many of the things that we know today as physical science were also once ideas or concepts considered to be metaphysical. As we evolve in our individual consciousness, so too will the collective consciousness evolve, giving rise for more concepts to be confirmed by science.

Hopefully, you are open to this or at least open to the idea that there is more going on than what science can explain. The next logical question is, "Then what is actually going on?" Unfortunately, I don't know that we can ever answer that question. Not completely anyway. But what we can do is confirm to ourselves that there is in fact something temporarily unexplainable, something else, at work here.

I am not encouraging anyone to read this and accept it as fact. Honestly, like any nonfiction work, all of these ideas should be challenged. What I am suggesting is that you keep an open mind to these ideas. Draw back on your own experiences and see if they match up with these concepts. Look within before determining your opinion on these concepts.

The rest of this book will focus on some key concepts surrounding life and spirituality. The information I'll cover is only meant to help and encourage, so when you read something that feels right, then great. If you read something that doesn't resonate with you or doesn't empower you, then leave it be. This is all information that I obtained through a series of meditations, observations, readings, and channelings that resonated deeply within my being (a long-winded way to say "journey"). I do not, and never will, have the answers to life's big (or even little) questions. All I have are my own insights gained through my experiences that I am fortunate enough to share.

Part Two

Awareness

"What is necessary to change a person is to change his awareness of himself." – Abraham Maslow

If you're still reading, I want to thank you for accompanying me on this journey off the deep end. Even as I write this, I can't help but say to myself, "So, you just explained the unexplainable by offering the explanation that it can't be explained." And before I check myself in to the psych ward (which maybe I'm in as your reading this since publishing takes a while), I have to be ok with that. I have to be ok with my own current limitations. Maybe in the future I will understand more. Maybe the future doesn't exist because time is only a perception of our human condition. Either way, I'm ok with that as long as I am aware of what I don't or can't currently understand.

Awareness is key to many things in life, but especially to emotional and spiritual growth. Our level of awareness has 100% affected every aspect of our growth and development up to this current moment in time (whether time exists or not). The simple fact that you are reading this now can attest to that. Whether the title of this publication drew your attention, a friend recommended it, or you are in fact one of my friends reading this to show support as I've seemed to be acting unpredictably lately and you want to deter me from offing myself (if you're the latter, thank you, but I promise I'm fine), your awareness of your own state of being got you here.

Awareness is a term we hear often, especially in the realm of spirituality or self-improvement, which are basically the same thing. Awareness is a state of being aware, obviously enough, but aware of what? Some would say the goal is to be aware of everything, but I think that's vague and seemingly unrealistic. What I think works better is trying to become aware of that which you previously were not. Trying to notice things that you don't usually notice.

If you're an over thinker like many, this may drive you crazy at first. Maybe you become aware that every time you hear something you don't like, you make a certain facial expression. As you become aware of this, you may wonder, "Did I always do this, or am I only doing it now as a result of trying to be aware of what I'm doing?" Try not to go too deep down that rabbit hole. Just be aware and move on. If this becomes annoying initially, then you're on the right path. When practicing this, you may feel the urge to immediately take action to correct something that you're aware of that you do not like. If that anxiety arises, try to seek comfort in the awareness that becoming aware was an action in itself.

Eventually, being aware that something annoys you will be enough of an action for your ego. You'll be able to observe that event, say to yourself, "Hmm, that annoys me," then let go of it instantly. Imagine how wonderful that would be, not needing to spend hours, days, weeks thinking about that shitty remark your boss made to you because of his insecurities. By simply by acknowledging that it happened and becoming aware of how it affected you, you will gain insight.

Not too long ago, my boss told me that I'm "a fucking piece of shit." Granted, that was beyond inappropriate, but I let it bother me for years. Years!!! Anger was my dominating emotional response to that event, and I just couldn't get over it. I could not let go because I never sought awareness, only revenge and a need to somehow prove the opposite. Through my own spiritual journey, I was able to revisit this occurrence and gain awareness into the reality of the situation.

When I became aware of how I really felt, I realized the anger was just a mask for fear. Fear that I was a fucking piece of shit. When I got honest with myself, I really wasn't the best employee at that time. I wasn't a fucking piece of shit employee, but awareness helped me see the situation honestly and with understanding for not only myself, but for my boss as well.

Awareness doesn't always need to lead to a revelation of insecurities. Sometimes, the perspective it gives us is enough to completely wash away a nagging thought. Being aware brings us into the now, and I'll discuss this more later, but there are zero anxieties or stressors in the now. You can't be upset about something that happened in the past once you become aware of the fact that it is 100% in the past. You can't be worried about the future when you become aware of the present. When you become aware of the present, you also become aware that the present is all that exists. It's the only existence we really have. But that's impossible to understand without practicing awareness.

So, how can one practice awareness? Well first off, let's all agree to make ourselves aware that it's likely a lifelong process with obscure boundaries that will be different for everyone, ok? Agreed. Next, let's throw some ideas out there and wing it like we always do. Sounds like a plan.

One of the most common practices when it comes to awareness is meditation. It certainly was my first step in developing awareness. I'm not sure if meditation gives you awareness or if you need to gain a sense of awareness in order to meditate, but either way, stumble in that direction and you'll probably make progress. Going hand in hand with meditation is breathwork. Many find that by focusing simply on their own breath, that they gain more control and can quiet the ego thus giving way to subtle awareness.

Since we can't always be in a state of zen-like meditation, it would be wise to develop the habit of being aware throughout your day-to-day activities as well. There's no one way to do this, but being present and in the moment will help you pay attention to what you're actually experiencing. Pay attention to the feelings you have and to your reaction to people, things, and explanations. If you're disciplined enough, keep a journal on them. What you may begin to find as your overall awareness grows is that you've been ignoring a lot of what you experience because you aren't always truly present.

Though it will seem difficult at first, which is typical of most new endeavors, it will become one of the easiest and healthiest habits you have. There's a certain freedom that awareness will bring you. You'll feel more in touch with your reality. And though you'll become aware of how little control you have over the universe, you will also become aware of how much control you have over how you react to the universe. Through that awareness comes a true sense of freedom.

Frequency

"If you want to find the secrets of the universe, think in terms of energy, frequency and vibration." - Nicola Tesla

The key to all things metaphysical (and physical...maybe I should've just said the key to all things) is frequency. Frequency refers to a specific vibratory rate of energy. For most schools of thought, everything comes back to energy. Everything is energy. Everything we experience as human beings, including the essence of being human, is energy. We tend to focus on mostly physical forms of energy like matter, light, and sound as those are the easiest forms for us to experience. Because the perception of these forms is painfully apparent to us, they become the cornerstone of our human experience.

One would think that since we experience things like solid matter every second of every day that it would be the easiest to understand, but that is not the case here. Absurdly oversimplifying it, the study of quantum physics breaks down units of matter. Everything boils down to atomic and subatomic particles, which are essentially different forms of energy or different vibratory rates. Now, my bachelor's degree in exercise science (yes, that's a thing) didn't really leave me with a firm grasp of the ins and outs of quantum physics; however, I benefit from the fact that humanity has been blessed with many gifted writers who have been able to eloquently explain such concepts so that the rest of us may understand. The biggest takeaway I have derived from these brilliant authors is that in physics, just like in many aspects of life, every answer seems to lead to even more unanswered questions.

For instance, let's look at matter. Matter is made up of atoms. Atoms are made up of subatomic particles like electrons and quarks. What subatomic particles are made of is a guess at best, so we'll stick to the atom. Essentially, the atom is made up of a nucleus with an orbiting electron. In between the two is "space." Fancy mathematics calculate that most of what makes up an atom (like over 99%) is dead space; they are essentially saying that all of something is made mostly out of nothing. Nothing that we currently understand how to perceive, anyway.

What I'm really driving at here is that we, as a society, just don't completely know what's going on. Not in a sense that we can prove tangibly or that all parties would agree on. But I'm not convinced that everything needs an explanation. Awareness can be just as, if not more, powerful. If, as individuals, we took the time to simply be more aware of what was happening in our own experiences, we would see distinct patterns in situations that correspond with our emotions in addition to our physical experiences. If our bodies are made up of matter, which holds a frequency, why wouldn't our thoughts and emotions also hold a frequency?

There are many books that talk about the law of attraction. Unlike this book, most of the aforementioned books are very well written and draw quotes from various religious texts to illustrate that the idea of the law of attraction has been around for a long time. When broken down, some of the specifics may vary from author to author, but essentially the idea is this: What you put out to the universe, via thought, emotion and action, is what the universe will give you in return.

Over time, I have heard quite a few arguments from people who are skeptical of this school of thought. I was certainly a skeptic myself when I was first introduced to this idea. It didn't make sense to me that I could change my circumstances simply by playing pretend in my head. Focus on the things I want, and they'd come? So I tried that, and obviously it didn't work, but that's because I didn't understand.

For whatever reason, the negative examples were easier for me to see, so as I became more aware of my own thoughts and tendencies, I could clearly see how I, and those around me, were using this universal law to generate negative outcomes.

My personal favorite, and the simplest (not a coincidence) example that is commonly used to explain this idea is that of a person who keeps saying, "I can't get a flat tire. I just couldn't afford a flat tire right now." Then, you guessed it, they get a flat tire. If you don't find that example to be realistic, please take a moment here and try to find a relevant situation that you have recently witnessed that is comparable this simple example. I'm sure you can come up with at least one (but likely many) similar example from either your own life or the lives of the people around you. Like the friend whose biggest fear is losing their significant other and they end up driving their partner away as a result. Or the asshole who is always bitching and moaning about how terrible his job is but doesn't understand why more terrible work-related occurrences keep coming his way (can you guess who I'm referencing?).

If this is you, no worries. This was me to a "T." Being that I'm a fucking human, I can certainly revert back to these negative thought patterns from time to time despite my best efforts. The key to overcoming this is first becoming aware. When you are aware of the thought patterns, you then gain the power to work on changing them. The simplest thing to do is to work some gratitude into your thought process.

Let's use the flat tire example. Nobody wants a flat tire, or any costly car related issue for that matter. Yet people attract them all the time. We will attract what we focus our mental energy on. Even if we are saying we don't want a flat tire, our focus is on a flat tire, so the universe gives us a flat tire. When the thoughts arise, creating fear because you don't think you can afford to have a flat tire, try to shift into thoughts of gratitude. Be thankful you have a car. Be thankful it got you wherever you had to go so far today or the day before. Be thankful you have a life where you need a car to get around. Be thankful for whatever you have going on that's worth being thankful for. The key is to focus only on things or feelings that you want. You want to be thankful because you want more situations that make you feel thankful.

When you focus on these favorable feelings, you begin to raise the frequency of your being to match that of the positive feelings. Because of the principles of resonance (the frequency of an object matching the frequency of a nearby object), you will then turn into a type of magnet in which you'll draw forth more situations and experiences that cause the favorable and positive feelings.

From my experience, the more one elevates their frequency and begins magnetizing the experiences they want, the harder it becomes for unwanted experiences to enter their space. It will be harder for low frequency occurrences to get to you if you are spending little to no time vibrating on their level. Unfortunately, this can work against someone who is consistently vibrating on a lower frequency. By remaining on a lower frequency, they can make it considerably harder for high frequency events to enter their space. Though initially they may find it harder to attract high frequency events, all negative vibrations can be undone over time.

The focus here is to try to elevate your frequency and spend time vibrating at the same frequency as your desired event. This can be done by trying to produce the emotions you would have if you were granted said desire. Several books suggest exercises where you visualize the things you want. Getting very specific, you think about what your life will be like once you have the new job, new house, new lover, etc. You spend time imagining exactly how you will feel once you have these things. You want to really experience these feelings so that you can attract experiences that render the same feelings.

Not exclusive to experiences or material possessions, this applies to the people we bring into our lives as well. As we strive to elevate our frequency, we attract those operating at a higher frequency. When we meet these people, we feel as if they are magnetized. We feel like we are being drawn to them, because we are. This is a two-way street, and those at a higher frequency will be equally drawn to us. By elevating us they elevate themselves, giving us the chance to elevate others. By elevating others, we elevate ourselves. It's a limitless cycle of growth and opportunity, just like life.

The success of using the law of attraction relies heavily on having faith, and this is where it gets tough for most people. No matter how thoroughly we trust that our desires are coming our way, we maintain an acute awareness of every moment that passes where our desires have not come. That awareness is our reality because it's what we are experiencing, and we unconsciously end up focusing on not having our desires. To have true faith is to simply put out the request and let it go, which sounds easy in theory but can be damn near impossible in practice.

Let's say you're focusing on improving your current employment situation. You have overcome all negative thoughts about your current position and begin to practice gratitude for the aspects of your job that you love. As a result of you amplifying this positive vibration and higher frequency, things at work do get better. Suddenly an announcement is made that a position is opening within your department, and you may have a shot at a promotion. Of course, this is it. This is a direct result of all the hard work and positive thinking.

Then the big day comes. The announcement is made, and you didn't get the job. You think, "Wait what? Why the fuck not? I did everything right! You are a liar! If you were a restaurant, your soup of the day would be bullshit bisque! I'm an idiot for even thinking that the law of attraction could get me anything, let alone a promotion."

That would be a very common thought process for someone who allowed themselves to dive back into the negative. That was my exact process at a time when I was passed up for a promotion that I thought I deserved. Luckily, I didn't allow myself to stay in the negative for too long, because what I didn't see coming was the even better promotion that I received a few months later. The promotion that I received was far better for me than the promotion I was originally butt-hurt about not getting.

Things didn't work out in a way that initially made sense to me or that I could predict, so I assumed things just weren't going to work out. The truth was that I didn't need to be able to see how things would play out. That's not my job in this. All I needed to do was remain open to receiving, and the universe took care of the rest.

Very rarely are the things we ask for going to be brought to us in a way that we can predict or that makes a lot of sense to us, and that's ok. Our role in this process is to let it happen. Ask, visualize, and then trust that it's coming.

Emotions as Feedback

"One ought to hold on to one's heart; for if one lets it go, one soon loses control of the head too." — Friedrich Nietzsche

If vibrational frequency is a universal force that is constantly at play, then surely we would have been given some mechanism to work with said frequency, right? Great question, skeptic mind. Low and behold, we have all been gifted with a wonderful, sometimes frustrating, and very complex feedback system to measure our resonance with vibrational frequencies. I am referring to our emotions. Having frequencies of their own, emotions are one of the mediums we use to interpret and interact with the frequencies surrounding us.

Through my own efforts to uncover my true self, I have realized that my emotional reactions to situations act as a guiding system for my spiritual journey. If I'm feeling content in any given scenario, I know it resonates closely to the frequency that I'm currently vibrating in. When I'm excited or happy, I know I'm in a situation that is pushing me towards a higher vibration. Anger jealousy, or any other negative emotions tell me that I'm lowering my vibrational frequency.

I'm not sure what the main goal is for one's life in terms of frequency, but my guess is that it has something to do with maintaining a very high vibratory rate. If you believe in a god, then a reasonable aspiration could be to vibrate as close to your god's frequency as possible. If you look at the teachings of the most prolific spiritual leaders (i.e. Jesus, Buddha, post-2010 Jim Carrey), you could infer that aligning with your inner presence (God-self, Holy Spirit, soul, etc.) would be a good aiming point. I won't refer to this alignment as *the* goal in life, but let's agree that it probably should be *a* goal, or at the bare minimum, an aiming point.

Ok, back to emotions. We feel a very broad range of emotions, some more than others; but in general, most emotions can be labeled as either positive or negative. When we experience situations or thoughts that promote positive emotions, then we are receiving feedback from the great creator that we are becoming more in tune with the frequency of our inner being. Something along the lines of, "Hey, you're not fucking things up too badly right now. Nice job!" When we experience thoughts or situations that bring about negative emotions, that's God letting us know that we are moving out of alignment with the frequency of our inner being. Something like, "LOL, you're doing it again. You're being too 'extra' right now" (if God was a millennial).

Some may argue, myself included, that this can't be true because sometimes it feels good to do bad things. On the very surface that can appear to be true, but to quote the great American poet Meek Mill, "There's levels to this shit". Our egos do amazing things, and too often one of those tasks is to disguise our true emotions with superficial emotions.

Bullying is currently a hot topic, so let's use that as an example. There is no dearth of viral videos titled "Bully Gets What He Deserves," or something similar. There's something seemingly satisfying about watching some punk talk all sorts of smack only to get embarrassed by the victim landing a knockout blow to the would-be villain. Initially, you might watch a video like this and feel good because the world seems a bit fairer now that justice has been served. But try watching one of these videos without the context of the intro. Watch only the part where someone is getting physically hit into unconsciousness. To take it a step further, realize that we are in a time where I am able to reference viral videos of children getting knocked unconscious and you know exactly what I'm talking about. Does any of this feel good?

Watching a stranger get maliciously attacked does not evoke positive feelings for most viewers. If the viewer is able to attach some notion of their identity to the attack, they may be able to cling to some falsely satisfying feeling; but even then, it is a hoax. For example, while watching a video of a man wearing New York Giants gear get knocked out, a Philadelphia Eagles fan might feel a twinge of happiness, not only because they are drunk at noon, but also because they are attaching to the premise of the something happening against a Giants fan. Essentially, their subconscious simplifies the video to, "Boo, Giants," which aligns with their version of reality, evoking a positive emotion through an affirmation of beliefs. It's not the physical harm that evokes the positive feeling, but the attachment to the idea that it promotes one's beliefs.

Another example that hits home for me is gossip, especially at work where I typically harbor a lot of resentment towards my bosses. Ironically, I am writing a book which specifically states that those resentments are only harmful to me, yet here we are. Sometimes, I find myself in conversations with my boss's boss and I end up sliding some super petty bullshit in the conversation, drawing attention to some negative thing my boss has done. Feeling that my boss had acted wrongly and gotten away with it, telling his boss about it is my only chance at enacting some accountability in this situation. Initially, I will feel good about this, almost brave, but more importantly, like I am taking action and righting the previous injustices that were unfairly thrust upon me.

Within an hour of that conversation, I will feel very not good. I will feel unsure, cowardly, and ultimately dishonest. So, what changed? Nothing really. Those emotions were always there, I just let ego put my pride in front of them. I know that I did not go about things in an honest way; rather, I chose to sacrifice integrity for convenience. Knowing at the time that wasn't the best way to approach things, I still chose to handle it in that way. The worst part is, those petty conversations yield very few positive results as well. All I did was put more strain on an already rocky relationship with my supervisor while undermining my own self-esteem in regards to being a good person. Needless to say, those situations have yielded plenty of emotional feedback, helping me realize that those actions were moving me away from my desired vibrational alignment.

Even if you can't relate to those examples, there has surely been a time where you hurt someone, either physically or emotionally, because you initially felt justified. I invite you to pick a time where this has happened and honestly think about it. After the initial sense of revenge, pride, or justice wore away, was the feeling you were left with a positive one? Even when the other parties are in the wrong, we will not gain any spiritual benefit from hurting them or taking from them. Our emotional feedback confirms this.

I now invite you to think back to a time where you were wronged and were able to truly forgive the other party without taking action against them. These memories may be a tad harder to recall, but you've definitely done it, so keep searching until you find one. Found one? Awesome. How did it feel to truly forgive, to truly let go and be completely unbothered by the situation? It's freeing, and our emotional feedback tells us that is who we really are.

The truth is, the universe has its own system to bring justice to those who wrong us. Call it karma, call it whatever you'd like, but trust that it's real and that it doesn't need you to do its job. On the flip side of that, when we are wronged, this typically means we brought it upon ourselves in one way or another (think back to the negative examples of the law of attraction).

Now please don't misinterpret this and think that every time you've been wronged it's because you deserved it. That's self-deprecation, and that's not good. Understand that every time you've been wronged, you've merely felt that you were wronged. Take solace in the fact that on a spiritual level, you have somehow asked for these seemingly negative experiences so that you could learn from them. If you can view these negative life events as lessons or challenges that your soul or spirit has asked for, your life in general will begin to appear much easier.

"What about people who've been raped or murdered? Did their souls ask for that?" asked uppity skeptic who constantly plays devil's advocate to mask his own ever-growing list of insecurities.

"Yeah, unfortunately, that's what I'm saying," replies a reluctant and grossed out aspiring author who desperately hopes to mask his own ever-growing list of insecurities. Look, those extreme examples are truly horrific and absolutely baffling to many of us when we read about them or, even worse experience them, either firsthand or through a loved one. As much as I love stirring the pot and making light of things, I could never, in good conscious, detract from the seriousness of experiencing such trauma. When I am suggesting that on a spiritual level, the victims brought those events into their life experience, I am suggesting only that. I am saying that as humans they did not exhibit any conscious control and thus are in no way responsible for experiencing such horrific events.

I am suggesting, however, that on a soul level, their spiritual essence agreed to be a part of the experience for one reason or another. Many in the metaphysical community would call such an agreement a soul-contract, and it works for both positive and negative life events.

This has to be a very hard pill to swallow for some. But to simplify, if you believe that God, the universe, whatever, is all-loving, then you have to believe that this all-loving force would not subject you to something that you didn't agree to at some level.

If you're still not on board, I understand. If you're upset or offended, I understand. If you still feel like this idea is putting blame on the victims, then I didn't do a good job of explaining what I'm trying to say here. What I am suggesting should only be empowering. It should free them by allowing them to take comfort in the knowledge that they experienced what they have for their own benefit, to learn what they were sent here to learn through overcoming their traumas. Regardless of the severity of the trauma, adapting this belief makes it much easier to move on from. And since we have yet to figure out how to transcend time, moving on is the only real way to undo whatever damage has been done.

Shit, that got kind of dark.

Ego

"Make your ego porous. Will is of little importance, complaining is nothing, fame is nothing. Openness, patience, receptivity, solitude is everything." — Rainer Maria Rilke

Until my journey into the spiritual community, I never stopped to think about what the "ego" is. I remember some attempts by others to define ego for me, like in psychology classes I've taken over the years, but none of that stuck with me. Like most, any time I heard someone mention the term ego, I thought they were referring to a personality trait, specifically, a tendency that a person has where they present themselves as cocky or arrogant.

Since my awakening, my concept of ego has changed immensely. Though I believe it contributes to the aforementioned trait, I have learned that our egos are much more. The ego is a part of us but also seems to have a will of its own. In the end, the ego is whatever you decide it is, because your experience is relative to your understanding. This is why many of us prefer to define ourselves as spiritual in lieu of identifying with a religious denomination. To identify as a member of a religion is relatively specific in regards to others' understanding of the term. Identifying as spiritual is specific enough to let others know that you feel a connection to something higher, but vague enough that they don't immediately assume you've been circumcised or think that you hate gay people.

I apologize for getting off topic for a moment, but since I brought this up, I must quickly address it. How did circumcision get tied into religion? Do people believe that God himself demanded this? How did that conversation go?

God: "Listen now, my child, as it is my will that you to take these words to your people. I will give thee a few simple rules by which those who wish to be in my graces can live."

Some Bro: "Yes, my Lord, I shall deliver the word of God."

God: "Very well, my child. First and foremost, don't murder each other."

Bro: "Of course, Master. That makes much sense. What else?"

God: "Rule two: Don't steal from each other. That's also not cool."

Bro: "Most uncool, my Lord. Anything else?"

God: "Well since you've asked, there is one more thing I need you to pass on, and it's a bit specific, so you'll need to pay attention."

Bro: "The utmost attention, Master."

God: "So, you know that little bit of extra skin that I put on the end very end of your penis?"

Bro: "Yes, Lord God, I know it quite fondly for I play with it a little every day."

God: "Yeah, about that, I'm going to need you and all of my followers to go ahead and just slice that off."

Bro: "Hmm. Well not to question the word of God, but..."

God: "Exactly, rule four is no more questions. Gotta go. This is the word of God."

That's almost certainly how it went down right? Anyway, back to ego. Ego is another word that can be a bit ambiguous to a reader, so to best understand what I'm laying out in this writing, please keep in mind that I'm simply referring to my concept of ego.

When I refer to the ego, I am talking specifically about an intangible part of our consciousness that is concerned primarily with the physical component of our existence. It's that part of us that turns the collective "we" into the singular "I." Certainly not a concept I understood right away (or at all), but by practicing awareness, I have begun to develop an understanding and acceptance of my own ego.

When I first realized that my ego was something more than an answer on a Psych 100 quiz, I viewed my ego as the bad guy. Later, I would see this as a misunderstanding, but in that moment, I had to use a label in order to develop an understanding. By looking at ego as the bad guy, I was able to give it context which allowed me to do more research and soul searching which then allowed me to develop a deeper understanding of the concept. Here's the catch to all of this — understanding is a mechanism for the ego.

70

If after reading that, your first thought is, "What the fucking fuck is this guy talking about?" then you've just had a firsthand interaction with your ego. This could be perceived as a frustrating or idiotic idea to entertain or as a rewarding or joyous revelation. That would depend on the context you've used to create your understanding. Quite ironically, I needed to view my ego as the bad guy in order to learn that it is not. Ego is a necessity. I can only speculate as to why ego exists as a necessity, meaning I can't really explain why we need a part of us that encourages us to act against our best interest at times. But I can rationalize that it is necessary simply because it exists. Because it is a necessity, it cannot be the "bad guy," nor can it be the "good guy." All the ego can be is the ego.

So far my ego has made writing this book exceedingly difficult. After each passage, it sends me a vivid scene where Jane Reader closes my book and proclaims, "That is a crock of horse shit served with bullshit garnish." If by any chance that is your actual reaction to this, then I hope you can at least appreciate that I took the time to add a garnish. Truth be told, that will likely be some peoples' reaction to reading this. But it won't be everyone's reaction. It most likely won't be the majority of readers' reactions, yet it is the only reaction that my ego feeds me. This could be dangerous if I only listened to my ego, or if I wasn't able to be aware of my ego. But since I am aware of it, I use it as a tool. Instead of a vehicle that inhibits action, I use my ego like a lighthouse that illuminates my fears and insecurities. I can't let the light blind me and force me to turn around; instead, I use the light to guide me through a potentially dangerous path. If my ego is a part of me and is telling me that people will think that what I'm writing is garnished horse shit, then does part of me think this book is horse shit? Not exactly, because our egos lack the courtesy to be honest with us. What my ego is really saying is, "You are afraid that *you* are garnished horse shit." And unfortunately, there are times when I have those thoughts about myself. But rather than accepting my ego's invitation to self-deprecation land, I can acknowledge those fears and take a look at what's really going on.

71

I know myself better than anyone, and even if I have done shitty things at times, I know that I am not horse (or any other animal) shit. If I'm not shit and my writing accurately reflects me, then my writing cannot be shit either. Through this rationalization, I can re-focus my efforts and extract the inherent mission statement and apply it to this writing. Now, instead of editing to make sure this isn't shit work, I am editing to make sure that this book accurately represents my intentions.

Summarizing that process, I was able use the ego's message of self-doubt to identify a fear that was holding me back. Awareness of the fear led to conquering of the fear by reiterating my purpose and establishing a focus. This focus now encourages and energizes me in my writing endeavors. Thus, the ego ended up helping me in my writing process.

When you can begin to recognize these actions by your ego, you can work on acknowledging those thoughts and then work through them. And it is very important that you do acknowledge them. I hear people give each other advice all the time. Something along the lines of, "Don't focus on those negative thoughts." At times and with the right understanding, that can be very useful advice. But when you just stop focusing without first gaining awareness and understanding, you end up only repressing or ignoring whatever bad thoughts/fears/anxieties have arisen. And because your ego is your ego, it assumes you stopped focusing on those thoughts because it was right all along. What's worse is that your ego then gives these negative thoughts and ideas a fast tracked route to your subconscious where they meet the other lies your ego has created over the years.

Here's how I imagine my ego working. I picture a fancy little soirée with an open bar, and all of these thoughts are hanging out together. Kind of like a "Go Fuck Yourself" ball. Here's what happens next:

I'm Fat: "You come here often?"

I'm Stupid: "Oh yeah, I'm a regular here. I'm surprised we haven't met before."

I'm Fat: "Well, I believe that there are no coincidences in the universe, so I'm sure we're meeting for a reason. As a matter of fact, I got invited to this party after Willie tried on a shirt that didn't fit the way he wanted it to."

I'm Stupid: "Oh Em Geeze! I'm here because trying on that shirt was such a stupid idea for him in the first place!"

I'm Not Good Enough: "I'm sorry for listening in, but I couldn't help but overhear. Such a small world. I'm the one who told him the shirt didn't fit right."

End Scene.

These thoughts are comfortable at this party you're throwing for them. They are having a great time, and they have no reason to leave. Total lingerers. This is why it is imperative that you acknowledge these thoughts. By acknowledging the negative thoughts, you are taking their power away. Look them in the eye. Tell them that you not only acknowledge their existence but that you are *thankful* for them. You've now created awareness.

So now that you've acknowledged these thoughts and even thanked them, what is the next step? Well, there is no one correct answer here (which means there is no one incorrect answer either), so find what works for you. Ultimately, you will want to find your own way to let them go. What has worked the best for me is creating a context for my ego that works against the ego. Essentially, I like to plunge these negative thoughts into their own existential crisis where they convince themselves that they do not exist. Use the ego to fight the ego.

In the example above, my ego told me that I wasn't good enough to wear a shirt that I liked because I was too fat, meaning I had to be stupid for thinking I could pull it off in the first place. If I ignore those thoughts, they'll never leave. Even if I'm not focusing on them presently, they won't go anywhere and I'll end up revisiting them at another time. Instead of ignoring them, I find context that makes them irrelevant.

Me: "People need to wear clothes, and you're people so that was really
awesome how you tried to find a shirt that you liked."

Also Me: "But it didn't fit because I'm too fat."

Me: "Actually, it didn't fit because it didn't fit. That's really the only reason."

73

Also Me: "So, I'm not too fat?"

Me: "Only if you want to be. It's relative to your perception, so it's your choice. Are you too fat?"

Also Me: "I don't think I want to be."

Me: "So you're not."

Also Me: "Shit, you're right. I'm not."

That example is glaringly simple, but sometimes so is life. Through this example, I also gain the insight that I am the one who defines what too fat is. I am only too fat if I decide that I am. This doesn't mean that I'm going to abandon my physical health and completely let myself go, but it allows me to become aware and not judge myself. If I become aware that I'm unhappy with my body in its current state, then I can do something about it. When I think I'm too fat to wear certain clothes, then I'm stupid and whatever other labels my ego wants to throw at me. By becoming aware, we gain insight into reality. We see things for what they are. Once we see things clearly, the guests at your ego party will politely see themselves out.

This may be difficult initially. Of course your ego won't want this party to end, and it will do whatever it can to stop the process of clearing out its guests. But even the most voracious partier understands that a party of one is not really a party. Once you've cleared house, you'll find that this process becomes easier to duplicate, and you'll be able to get to the insight much quicker when this practice becomes a habit.

Though seemingly complex, this concept of ego becomes much simpler when broken down. Though it took me a considerable amount of contemplation and reflection, the simplest definition of ego that I can come up with is that it is a disguised synopsis of our fears. Tying that into my old definition of ego, when someone is bragging or coming across as a bit too full of themselves, I now see it as a confession of that person's fear. For instance, someone who is bragging about how much money they make is most likely bragging about how insecure they are about their ability to accumulate money. It could be directly related to a fear about someday losing their money. It could be that they are insecure about a perceived shortcoming that has nothing to do with income, but they believe their ability to accumulate money can compensate for that.

At one point or another, we are all guilty of this type of egotism. We use social media to brag about community service or our recent weight loss or how great we are at relationships when all we really want is some sort of validation. Becoming aware of this tendency in others will certainly help you show more patience towards the braggers. You can see their confession for what it is and respond with understanding rather than judgement.

Whether in ourselves or those around us, awareness and understanding are the great neutralizers for ego. Awareness grants us insight into the fear. Understanding grants us the ability to overcome the fear. With these tools, ego becomes a promoter of growth rather than the great inhibitor it would rather be. You can now be thankful for your ego for when it shows up unexpectedly in your life, it is presenting an opportunity to take another step closer to being the person you want to become.

Reality

"Reality is merely an illusion, albeit a very persistent one."- Albert Einstein

What the fuck is reality?

Good question. Reality itself can be a relatively broad term, and like any word, it can carry different meanings depending on the audience. Fatefully, that's similar to reality itself, where each person's reality is specific to them. It's the culmination of one's experiences that determine how they perceive the next. Everyone's reality is unique to them and is ultimately what one wills it to be.

Playing off the great unknown, some of the most popular modern mythologies provoke great introspection on the topic by making us question our own concept of reality. The most notable story of its kind, the 1999 film *The Matrix*, had entire generations nervously wondering if everything they knew was, in actuality, a computer simulation. One moment, you're sitting in your chair enjoying some popcorn and knowing, without any doubt, that you are a human being; then in an instant, one clever twist in a Hollywood blockbuster has you wondering if you're a computer program.

What if you are a computer program? Does that matter at this point? Would it actually change anything about your reality? You would still exist in the same way you always have. Nothing would be different except now you see yourself as a computer program. Essentially, it would not matter unless you decided you wanted it to matter.

Religions try to define reality for us in the simplest terms possible by providing us with purpose or, at least, a direction. But is the picture they paint much different from that of a modern video game? Christianity provides the concept of heaven (you win) and hell (you lose). You're born, you level up, and then you complete a series of quests hoping to solve them the way the great game developer in the sky intended. Eastern religions that promote the concept of reincarnation are not much different, except they let you pop in the game genie so you can play with unlimited lives.

But essentially, it's still a game, albeit a longer one. Maybe this is why we are drawn to stories like *The Matrix*. Not because they confirm our perceptions of reality, but because they remind us that we can never really know for sure the true nature of our reality.

So, what is reality? I sure don't know. And I don't know that we as a species will ever come to a conclusion on this that satisfies the collective ego. Part of our reality is coping with the fact that we'll never fully understand it. Paradoxically, isn't knowing that we can't understand our reality actually a way of understanding it? Yes. Understand that you can't understand. Then move on.

The frustration that one can never solve the puzzle is enough to keep most from ever attempting it, yet freedom from the knowledge that there is no answer has encouraged many to unlock wonderful and previously unfathomable secrets in their quests for more knowledge. One reality, but two different outcomes. If there is such a thing as the human condition, this is it for me. Perspective.

The beautiful part of having free will is that it enables us to choose how we want to perceive our reality. Once we decide that the big questions are unanswerable, we can choose how we let that frame our own perspective. Essentially, we get to choose our own realities. Because I will never know the answer, I can tell myself that there's no point in trying to figure it out since it is impossible to figure out. Or I can see it as more of a freebie. Since it's impossible to know the true meaning of life, there is no wrong answer. Personally, I prefer the latter.

A person who decides that because there is no real answer, there is no need to look for one is severely limiting themselves in terms of potential. That is a person who will undeniably be wrapped up in the goings on of the ego and will find ways to perpetuate that part of their existence. It could be through drugs and alcohol, toxic relationships, vanity, whatever. Oftentimes people may simply just choose to be miserable fucks. You know people like this. Chances are you've been like this yourself; God knows I have. I've tried all of those examples. Many times.

Now let's look at the other side of things — the person who understands that they'll never fully understand. They love that there is no answer, yet they acknowledge that the fact that there is no answer is an answer in itself. Then they become elated by the fact that none of that makes any fucking sense at all. You know people like this. Chances are you've been like this yourself. I strive to be that person.

How you choose to look at things will greatly affect every aspect of your life. In fact, it's been affecting you since you were born and will continue to do so until you die. Maybe even after, depending on what your reality is then.

One of my favorite examples of this occurs every day with young children. You've done this as a child and you've probably been on the other end of this as well. A little boy is running around, being a kid, and he falls. Maybe he scrapes his knee, maybe it's nothing. It's usually nothing. But he looks for the nearest adult to figure out how he should respond. He's looking for context. He makes eye contact with his father who is anxious and worried that his child hurt himself under his watch. The boy starts bawling. He chose this reaction.

A little girl is running around, being a kid, and she falls. Maybe she scrapes her knee, but maybe it's nothing. It's usually nothing. She looks for the nearest adult to try to figure out how to respond. She makes eye contact with her mother who is grounded in reality and virtually unfazed by the said event. She is aware that it was nothing. Observing no reaction, the daughter chooses to get up as if nothing happened and continues to play.

Both children experienced the exact same event, yet they yielded entirely different outcomes. Why is this? Perspective. Children are much more aware of the nonphysical realm of our existence and much less concerned with physical side of existence. They are "new" to existing in the physical realm, so their ego is still in its infancy. This is why most will look to others to gauge what their reaction should be, if any. The truth is, physically, the fall is not that painful. However, such an event could be very painful to one's sense of pride, which is tied into the ego. The child who is coddled by a worried father is actually getting his ego strengthened, whereas the little girl whose mother was unfazed was able to act purely on the reality of her situation.

So were the little boy and his father wrong in that situation? No. There is no wrong and there is no right. There is only our perception which shapes our events into our reality. In that example, the father's reality is that he was worried because he was focused on things other than the actual event. Had he been focused simply on the fall, specifically the lack of injury it produced and not what it could mean as a reflection of his own parenting ability, the outcome would've been different.

Disclaimer: If while reading the above example you felt resentful or guilty because you've been in that exact situation, acknowledge it and let it go. Don't let your reaction or perspective distract from the message. The truth is that we've all played out each of those roles at one point or another in our lifetimes.

It is generally easy to understand these concepts when we can see it in fictional examples or in other people. It is much more difficult, however, to see these tendencies in our own actions. Unfortunately, regardless of how grounded or spiritual someone may be, they will have to deal with a harmful or negative perspective from time to time. For many of us, it's little things. We look at traffic like it's the universe waging a personal war against our lives and happiness, though we could choose to look at it as more alone time to listen to podcasts or music. If you're not alone in the car, then it could be an opportunity to get to know someone else better. If you don't want to get to know that person better, then it's an opportunity to study your own ego and judgements to figure out why you feel that way. The bottom line is that traffic is traffic. You were well aware of its existence before you departed on your trip. You probably even expected that you would encounter it on your drive as we usually know when and where traffic will arise. So, what's the actual problem then? Yup, you guessed it — your perspective.

Perspective

"There are no facts, only interpretations"- Frederick Nietzsche

If reality is the picture, then perspective is the frame. At the most immediate level, we have seen examples of how perspective can influence or possibly manifest different outcomes. Most would agree that in the previously discussed events in which the children fell, the individual perspectives of the participants had a direct effect on the outcome. Those that don't agree, I am confident, could devise their own real-world example that would illustrate the same point. It's not an exceedingly difficult concept to understand. The difficulty comes in finding it, even though it's hiding in plain sight.

Part of our human condition is that even though we understand concepts on a small scale, we seem to choose to be ignorant to the fact that the same rules must be true on a large scale. For example, if someone were to use a gasoline powered generator, they would instinctively make sure that they didn't run it indoors or in a closed setting. They know that that would be harmful to their health as the fumes are toxic. However, that same person would seldom consider that the fumes could be harmful to the environment. We know the gasoline fumes are deadly in a closed room. But since they aren't deadly in open air, we barely think about it when a car drives by us in a parking lot, or when we're sitting on the 405 freeway surrounded by hundreds of other cars all pumping out the same toxic fumes. Because there is no immediate threat, our perspective about the threat from the fumes changes.

Because of our human condition, we have limited ways to observe experiences on the physical plane. It is easy for us to observe the effects that something could have on the atmosphere of a room because we generally experience it directly. Simply by turning off a light, talking, or lighting a candle someone could quickly change your direct experience in a room by adding these stimuli. These are all easily observed from the human perspective. The human perspective is governed largely by ego.

Then we have the nonphysical perspective. This is directly related to the intangible part of our existence, the part of us that we know exists, but can't really explain in terms that our ego wants to understand. Very often, when trying to explain this, the example used is walking into a room where an argument has just occurred. Even though you aren't aware of it physically by seeing or hearing it, there is a part of you that can sense the tension in the room. That part of you is your nonphysical being, or your spirit.

Our perspective in this situation determines what we label the cause of this phenomenon. One who has framed their reality with the idea that there is no existence beyond the physical plane will rationalize that they observed cues from body language to hypothesize that there was just an argument. They will hold on to that pattern of rationalization until their experiences show them otherwise. Everyone experiences forms of sensation through their nonphysical aspect of their being, but if they don't believe that there is a nonphysical aspect to their being, then it will always be rationalized away based on that individual's understanding.

As I've previously stated, I was one of these people until I was able to change my perspective on how I viewed the idea of a nonphysical existence. I didn't start out by completely switching my opinion and accepting the nonphysical; I merely needed to be open to the idea that there was more going on than I previously thought. That allowed me to experience one event after another until I received a very clear confirmation that there is a nonphysical aspect to my existence.

I talked about some experiences in the "Awakening" chapter, but probably the most intense experience I've had that was an affirmation that there is more than meets the eye happened when I practiced Reiki for the first time. While at my level one Reiki training, we got to the part of the day where we were going to practice on each other. One of the women there volunteered to be the first receiver of the Reiki energy and hopped on the table. It was a small group, and most of us believed that Reiki was real (Why else would we be at the training?) but none of us had "felt" the energy before, and I think we were all a bit skeptical. I know I was.

So this brave woman lies on the table, and the teacher tells us to start out with a scan. Just run the hand up and down the midline of the body to see what area is "asking" for the energy. I've run my hands over lots of things in my day and have never felt any energy that I'm aware of. I don't think I'm going to feel it, but I do as I'm told. Starting at the crown, I slowly make my way down, scanning each chakra as instructed. Crown, third eye, throat, heart. Nothing. Then I get to the solar plexus chakra, and I immediately understand why this woman went first. I could feel the energy radiating from her life force chakra. It was incredible how much energy was coming out of this tiny woman. And what's more incredible is that I could feel it. I was in amazement but wanted to play it cool, so I continued my scan and moved down to the last two chakras and felt nothing. Still a bit in disbelief, I decided I would work my way back up the midline just to make sure I wasn't imagining things; sure enough, I felt her energy again in the exact same spot.

The more we practiced that day, the more I was able to truly feel the currents of energy that are part of our beings. Energy that only hours before I didn't think existed. I don't believe that there is anything special about me that allowed me to feel it. I'm not more receptive to these energies than anyone else. But I was open to it, and then it happened.

In trying to get some of my friends to feel their own energies, I've encouraged them to try a few different methods. One exercise that some of my friends have found success with in consciously feeling this energy is by focusing their awareness on one part of their body. I think the hands work best. So, if you're up for it, take a moment to quiet your mind. Take some deep breaths to relax and fall into a meditative state (whatever that may mean to you). Then put all of your attention, all of your awareness, to the middle of one of your hands. Don't touch it with anything, just focus on it. Without letting your mind wander, without thinking about how ridiculous this is, just focus on it. Did you feel it? What is it, anyway? I don't really know how to explain it, but when I practice this exercise, I can feel the energy of my hand. Not my hand itself, but its essence. If you didn't feel it, don't worry. You may feel it another day, or you may feel something entirely different but relevant to your experience and your journey. I doubt that everyone who attends a Reiki training receives immediate confirmation as I did; that's just how it happened to work for me.

That experienced changed my perception. It changed how I viewed the body. It changed how I viewed other people. It changed how I viewed myself. And it was all because of how I chose to interpret my experience. I chose to believe that what I felt was Reiki energy. I chose to change my perspective. Someone else could experience the exact same sensation but choose to perceive it as something different.

Your perspective is the key to what you experience, so don't develop a perspective that inhibits your personal growth. If you think everything happens for a reason, then it does. If you think everything happens by pure chance, then it does. If you think you will get some helpful information out of this book, then you will. If you think this book is bullshit, then it is. Your reality is whatever you choose it to be so choose a perspective that serves you.

If something bad happens to you, how do you know it's bad? Your perspective tells you that it is. Now I'm telling you that you choose your perspective. So, why choose to perceive anything as bad? This concept is much easier said than done, but pick up any self-help book that's made the Best Sellers list in the past decade and you'll see the same principle written in a different way.

That's because successful people don't choose a negative perspective. They can perceive rejection and other challenges as opportunities to overcome. Think about this. What if the worst thing that happened to you today was now actually a powerful lesson that will benefit you in the long run? Is that a better choice for you? If you think so, then choose that perspective. Choose a reality that empowers you.

In the Now

"Realize deeply that the present moment is all you ever have." - Eckhart Tolle

As with most things in life, the simplest solutions are typically the most beneficial and are often the most difficult to achieve. That being said, in looking to improve one's life, the simplest yet most difficult skill that can be learned is the ability to be fully in the now. Being in the now? What does that even mean? Be present. Be aware of what you are experiencing right now in this very moment. It's a very simple concept but not necessarily easy to execute. For instance, right now you are reading. To be in the now, all you have to do is read. Point your eyes at the paper and let your brain do the rest. That's it.

If you are offended by something that you read or, perhaps more likely, you feel bored because you think the author is a no-talent whack job, then you are not present, not in the now. You're not wrong either, but you're definitely not present. If you are offended, you are likely focusing on some part of your ego that felt challenged by a sentence in this book. If you're bored, chances are your focus has drifted to other things that you could/should be doing. If you're completely present, then you're reading. When you're driving and you hit traffic and your anxiety takes hold of you, you are not in the now. That's your ego taking control and turning your focus to the future — what could be, not what is. At that moment, you are not late. You're 100% fine, so be fine. Most likely, being late is not the end of the world anyway; but if you want to be stressed about it, be kind to yourself and at least wait until you are actually late to get stressed! Besides, it's not actually being late that is upsetting, it's the potential of the consequences that we might face as a result.

Our egos do this to us all the time. We get sad or depressed on our way to work because we tell ourselves we don't like our jobs. We're not even at work yet, but we're telling ourselves we don't want to be there. The truth may be that you don't like your job, but if you're still going to go, the best thing you can do for yourself is be present. By being present, you will assuredly notice more of the small things about your job that you do enjoy. You will develop a healthier perspective towards your situation and likely gain insight into what you can do to change it.

One of the most common issues people in today's world deal with is anxiety. But what is anxiety? Anxiety.org says, "Anxiety is the reaction to situations perceived as stressful or dangerous." Anxiety is a reaction to our perception. It isn't the situation that causes the anxiety; it's our reaction, or one's perception, of a situation. If you are able to be 100% present and in the moment, it would be impossible to feel anxious unless you were presently in physical danger.

Example time. Your coworker invited you to a party and you said you'll go. You're on your way, and you begin to feel anxious that you won't know anyone besides your coworker. You start imagining different scenes of how this party could go for you, both good and bad. Then as you are walking to the door, you get a text from your coworker saying she can't make it. You're overcome with terror. There's no way you could go in now. You don't belong there. Everyone would think you were a complete weirdo for showing up to a place where you know nobody. You need to leave. Before you can retreat to your car, the door opens. But instead of a stranger, it's an old classmate. Someone you haven't seen in years. You had no idea she was friends with your coworker. Inside, you even run into a couple of other former classmates that you haven't seen since school. You spend the rest of the night catching up and marveling at what a small world it is. You have a great time.

Since it was a hypothetical situation, I suppose there could also be an example where everything goes to shit and it was the worst night ever, but what kind of psychopath would even bring that up? The point of that story is that you don't know what's going to happen. You can only know what is happening. In that example, anxiety almost lead to you missing a great time. Were you wrong in thinking that people would think you are weird for showing up at a party where you don't know anyone? The answer is, it doesn't matter. The reality was that the people in the party weren't even strangers. You only perceived them to be. Something to be aware of about perception: When it isn't based on the present moment, it distracts us from what actually is. In that scenario, up until the door was opened, your reality was that everyone inside was a stranger. Our perceptions make our realities.

Here's an example from my life. A few months ago, I was transporting a new student to from the Los Angeles area to the school I work for that is outside of Philadelphia. He was a young Hispanic gang member who had spent the last few years in and out of juvenile halls and group homes. While we were trapped in the plane and somewhere over Oklahoma, he started having a bit of a breakdown. After asking question after question, he all of the sudden goes off on the topic of physical restraints. We weren't talking about that, but clearly it was on his mind.

There in seats 22D and E, this kid starts losing his shit on me about how he's not going to let staff restrain him. We are already quite the odd couple as I am painfully white and clearly not this kid's relative, so I immediately get worried about drawing too much attention. I'm trying to explain to him that getting restrained only comes about if it is necessary. Some type of wisdom like, "If you don't want to get restrained, don't act like someone who needs to be restrained." He's not really letting the info sink in, and it's escalating.

He responds with, "Naw, man, fuck that. If staff tries to put their hands on me, I'ma jump off on them."

I've dealt with similar situations before when I taught these kids in formal classes, and it's usually not too stressful for me. But the fact that we were in this plane created the perfect storm for my anxiety to take hold. In this very moment, this young man is extremely angry. Balled fists, talking in a loud tone. Simply put, he's not having it. I begin to worry that he's about to jump off on me and I'm going to have to restrain him and the plane will have to land somewhere that's not Philly. And if that happens, we are going to make the news. And if we make the news, it's going to make me and my employer look really bad and I will surely be fired. If I'm fired, I'll likely be homeless by the end of the month. Then it dawns on me. I'm not present. And neither is this kid. None of the things that were happening in our heads were actually happening to us, yet the emotional responses were quite real.

Once I became present and in the moment, I was ready to deal with what was happening. Very calmly, I told this young man, "Look, I understand why you're concerned, but I don't think we should focus on that right now." I realize that in this moment, we are passengers on a plane, our job is to be flown somewhere, so I focus on that and say, "You know, I bet when you were getting cuffed and put in that cop car, you never thought it would lead to you taking your first flight."

Thank God that worked. I didn't discount his feelings and frustrations, but I redirected his focus and his reality to the present. Within seconds, he was a different kid. He even thanked me for giving him the opportunity of attending the school we were heading to. I wasn't able to dissolve this potential disastrous situation because I am some type of Jedi guru, though that would be badass. All I did was reconnect to the present. It gave me the insight to help my travel companion do the same. (The kid in this example successfully graduated the program I worked for and never once got restrained while he was there.)

When you are able to live in the moment and become fully present, you give up the need to perceive how situations could play out. You simply don't need it. It would be like sitting in a movie theater and not paying attention to the movie on the screen because you're trying to map out how the story will unfold. That could certainly be a fun game to play, but you'd never know what was actually happening on screen. Even if you guessed the right outcome, you'd never know it without actually watching the movie. You'd have to spend more time and money later to find out. Or troll your Facebook for spoilers, but why not just pay attention in the first place?

That's kind of how anxiety and perceptions work. They take our energy and focus away from what's really happening in the now. How many times have you had a full conversation with someone only to realize at the end you barely recall what you talked about because your thoughts were elsewhere? Perhaps you're focused on an email you need to respond to when you get back to your computer. Once you're at your computer, you are having a hard time focusing on your email because you feel guilty for not giving your friend your full attention during the conversation. If you're going to have a conversation, then do that. Just that. If you're going to write an email, then do that.

This is something that is hard for all of us in today's world. With increasingly amazing technology, we have everything at the touch of a finger. Life has become so fast that we worry about losing things we haven't even gotten yet. We worry so much about what people could think that we seldom take the time to find out what they do think. Those problems do not exist in the now.

When you are fully present, you can always give your full attention to the task at hand. Once this becomes normal practice, you will find that you are immediately better at every task you take on. It would be impossible for this not to happen. In the now, you will find that you no longer have a need for anxiety and worry. You will be amazed at how quickly the quality of your life and happiness will improve once you can put this in to practice.

Relationships

"The meeting of two personalities is like the contact of two chemical substances: if there is any reaction, both are transformed." — C.G. Jung

Relationships are tricky, so tricky, in fact, that I tried really hard to not write anything about them. I tried to convince myself that it wasn't my place or that I was unqualified. Both may be true, but nevertheless, the force that has guided me along this journey has been adamant that I include the topic. So, here we go.

I have come to learn that relationships can lead to the most wondrous experiences in human existence. I have also seen and participated in situations where relationships seemed to be the most powerful source of pain and suffering. So what's really going on here?

Well, at the core of our existence, relationships will always be present. In addition to lovers, family, and friends, we foster relationships with coworkers, clients, service providers, whomever. Relationships must be at the core of our existence. If this wasn't true, then we wouldn't live in an existence that is overflowing with other beings. We even have relationships with things. Inanimate objects (objects that we perceive to not be alive) can foster emotional attachments in us as well. Because relationships are at the very epicenter of our existence, they tend to have the most power over us and our experiences.

This power means that relationships can be dangerous. Not necessarily by nature, but by what our ego encourages us to do in regards to relationships and identity. Part of our human condition is that we always are trying to define ourselves. This can be great when we have ascended to a higher frequency and we begin to define ourselves as part of a God-conscious or universal energy. The most enlightened beings view themselves as a part of everything, and not a self at all. But before we get there, we tend to stick labels on ourselves in an attempt to answer the very hard to answer question: Who am I? It can sometimes feel safer to have the wrong answer than no answer at all.

Drawing an example from my own life, I have many times referred to myself as an asshole in defense of my actions. I remember specifically doing this with my boss one day after getting in an argument with a different supervisor in our company. Out of frustration, I said some things that were very true but were not very helpful to the situation. Instead of explaining the complex range of emotions I had been feeling as a result of pouring every ounce of my being into my job only to be told I was clueless and ungrateful, I called myself an asshole. I chose to undermine my own feelings because it was easier at that time to label myself than to deal with the uncertainties and ambiguities of my reality.

These labels become more dangerous with more meaningful relationships. I recently had a conversation with a friend in his 40s who labeled himself a failure because he had been divorced twice. Seeing as his primary social circle was comprised of married men similar in age and social status, he tied his marital status into his perception of self. What's worse, most of the advice he was getting from these people was making him feel worse. The advice consisted of generic comments like, "Marriage is hard work." Of course it is. It's a complex relationship that's success or failure is accompanied by serious social ramifications. Relationships are hard without the pressure of it affecting other aspects of your life, but I don't believe that's what was really being said to my friend. The truth is that the people saying this were only affirming what they have experienced. Here's a breakdown:

What they said: "Marriage is hard work."

What they meant: "My marriage is hard work."

What my friend heard: "Marriage is hard work, and you couldn't cut it."

He let other people build a mold that he didn't fit in, then he blamed himself for not fitting in it. We do this to ourselves in so many aspects of our lives that it can become exhausting to sort through. But awareness is the first step to change which is the precursor to growth.

Now, I am not suggesting that you don't talk to your friends when you're going through hardships. As I mentioned earlier, I believe relationships to be the backbone of our existence. I am suggesting that you make yourself aware of any labels you may be trying to stick on yourself before you have these conversations.

When it comes to relationships, just as in life, the key to happiness will come when we are most in tune with our true selves. This means fostering relationships that encourage us and affirm us in our existence. No long-term good will come out of relationships where partners believe they can fix the other, or even worse, that they can be fixed. Enter the infamous codependence.

There's a ton of literature published that discusses codependency. There are books written by psychologists than can offer a much more clinical insight on the topic than I could comprehend. But I do want to quickly touch on the concept in terms of a spiritual existence. When codependence arises, partners are tying their identity and perception of self into someone else's existence. Though there are many questions surrounding our existence, here's a little known fact that we can all agree on: Only you can exist as you. When your perception of your existence depends on the existence of another, you start to vibrate on a frequency that is different from your true self, inner-self, God-self. Initially, your ego may tell you this is great because it can take some pressure off of you and the decisions you make. You put the responsibility of your happiness in someone else's hands.

Why is this good? Well, it's not. But why be unhappy and additionally mad at yourself for allowing it when you could be unhappy but able to say, well at least it's not my fault? Those "enlightened" already know that in both scenarios, we are responsible for our own happiness, but our good pal ego will do its best to convince us otherwise.

Not only is hinging your happiness on your partner unhealthy for you, but it can also be equally damaging to your partner and ultimately the relationship. When one partner takes on this role of happiness generator, they begin to make decisions for themselves based on what they think their partner would like. This can also feel temporarily relieving as it indirectly reflects responsibility and ego-fueling control, though this is equally dangerous. It is always important to be considerate of your partner when making decisions, but they can't be the major factor. Ultimately, when one makes decisions for someone else, they take themselves out of tune with the frequency of their inner being or the essence of who they really are.

If this seems selfish to you, I get that; but try to look at it differently. To truly honor your relationship and your partner (and the universe and your existence for that matter), you owe it to them to be the best version of yourself. In order to be the best version of yourself, you will be required to have some scarily honest conversations that may seem uncomfortable at the time, but will ultimately be beneficial to all involved in the end.

There's an old adage that is wonderfully true which states that you cannot love someone until you learn to love yourself. To take that a step further, it is impossible to love yourself if you are not *being* yourself.

Spirituality

"Make your own Bible. Select and collect all the words and sentences that in all your readings have been to you like the blast of a trumpet." — Ralph Waldo Emerson

Since I'm writing a book about spirituality, I thought it prudent to explain my definition of spirituality. My favorite part about the term "spirituality" is that, like every other topic I've covered, it is incredibly vague and tends to carry different definitions depending on who you're talking to. This is probably another reason some people are hesitant to have these conversations. It is hard to have a conversation about something that is so loosely defined because it is hard to know how to be right in said conversation. From my experience, it is impossible to be right or wrong in discussing matters of spirituality. Unfortunately, that is not always the accepted viewpoint. Hopefully, this book can help promote that perspective, or minimally promote some type of understanding to different belief systems.

For all intents and purposes (or "intensive purposes," which is what I said until I was finally corrected at the age of 25), when I refer to spirituality, I am talking about the act of living our lives. I'm talking about our connection to our own lives and the people that we invite into them. It took me a while to adopt this view, but now I can't see things any other way.

Many people hear the term "spirituality" and immediately associate it with religion. For some, these topics may be closely tied together, but for most, these will be two separate ideas. For some, religion may provide a framework or game plan to develop a sense of connectedness, but spirituality would be the day-to-day execution of trying to follow that plan. Some feel that they need religion in order to have a sense of spirituality. In order to exist, religions need the concept of spirituality. Luckily for many, spirituality does not need religion.

Find whatever works for you, and go for it. Start your journey. Anything new will be hard in the beginning, but you're ready. Luckily, growing spiritually is difficult in appearance only, mostly because no one really knows exactly what "spirituality" means. In order for you to discover your own sense of spirituality, you need to define it for yourself. Seriously, that's the only way you're going to have a completely authentic and fulfilling understanding. Expose yourself to as much information as possible and take in as many experiences as possible. You will need many teachers along the way, and they will appear when you're ready for them. Take it all in, but only keep what feels right to you.

If you are currently devout in your religious practice and this sounds scary, it shouldn't be. If you truly have faith in your religion, then this will only strengthen your beliefs. If it raises questions, then you'll have some insight into where you need to find some answers. But ultimately, if you're practicing a religion that does not resonate with who you really are, then you may be holding yourself back from learning more about yourself. But like I said, you need to do what works for you, and you most certainly shouldn't make any life changes solely because I'm suggesting it.

Spirituality develops when we find ways to vibrantly display our true selves to the world. It's not about getting on our knees and saying thanks for things while asking for more things, though that may be part of it. Spirituality is about tapping in to our divine gifts and abilities. Everyone has something that they are truly gifted at. Everyone has a few things they are divinely adept at. Your spiritual journey should be about tuning in to those gifts and exploring them and figuring out how to use those gifts to better the lives of those around you.

I'm not implying that you should quit your job so you can completely focus on your gifts, whatever they may be, but I am suggesting that you take the time to figure out what those gifts are. Your job may be one of the best tools you have in deciphering your own gifts. Look at the parts of your job that you really love, the tasks that you get swept up in with no concept of time. The work that doesn't feel like work at all. Chances are, some aspect of those tasks are involving the deepest and truest parts of your being.

If you're still not sure what your gifts may be, ask your closest friends and family and, while you're at it, tell them what you think their gifts are as well. If they tell you something that doesn't feel right, then don't explore it at that time. Someone will say something that resonates with you and gives you a starting point.

Starting this journey is much more important than figuring out the destination. I can assure you that the idea of your perceived gifts will change immensely as you dive deeper into your quest for self-discovery. But you'll be changing as well. Embrace it and enjoy it. Whatever your divine gifts may be, get creative in incorporating them into your daily life as much as possible. If you can work it into the job you already have, then do that. If you can't, then put some time aside in your personal life, even if it's only five minutes, to explore the activities that you love.

Explore all possibilities, and don't procrastinate. You'll know you're on the right path by how you feel when you're doing these things. These activities will wash away the other stresses in your life. They will bring you excitement, challenge, joy, and most importantly, peace. Inner peace will bring you that sense of calm and understanding that allows you to help others. It will bring you a perspective that enables you to shed a positive light on any negativity around you. That inner peace is your compass to spirituality. Follow it.

Love

This is my epilogue and the shortest chapter. Hopefully, it's also the simplest. But of all that I've learned on my journey thus far, it is this: Love is the answer. Perhaps I could've saved us both a lot of time by putting this in the beginning, but that wouldn't have been nearly as fun. Plus, I don't think anyone would feel good about buying a one-page book.

Love is universal. It has no stipulations. No conditions. It is free. It is for everyone. It is everything.

In the end, regardless of the question, the answer is always love. All the topics I've covered and every experience I've laid out in this book can be boiled down to love. Whatever problems you have that you are currently dealing with, love is the answer. Whatever conflict you see in the world around you can be traced back to a lack of love and can be solved with love. Love is the magical, universal force, and it is the only thing in this existence that increases in magnitude the more you give it away.

Most of us never take the time to love ourselves, making it impossible to truly love others. What's worse is that this will also block us from receiving the love that others try to give us.

We live in a world that encourages us to label, judge, and file everything into categories that make sense to us. But what if, instead, we just loved? Love everyone. Love the guy that cut you off. Love the "God hates fags" people. Love the stranger that stole your identity and emptied your savings count, not just the bank agent that helped you get the money back.

It's such a simple fucking concept but by far the hardest to apply to one's life. But love yourself enough to try it. It's the secret ingredient to the recipe of life. This one-page cook book from the great creator could read as follows: When in doubt, add love.

And with that, I must bid you a great farewell. Thank you for embarking on this great journey with me, and I wish you the best of luck as you continue yours.

Much Love,   The Millennial Prophet ;-)

About the Author

Willie is an average Joe/Jolene and believes that is what makes his writing relatable to a broad range of readers. He is a loving father who hopes he isn't fucking up his children too much (more than the normal amount). He has worked a myriad of jobs and dabbled in several genres of hobbies throughout his 35 years on this planet. Professionally, he spent over a decade working as a teacher and counselor for at-risk youth from the roughest cities in the country before pivoting to a sales and marketing role which focuses on helping small business owners increase profitability.

Outside of his LinkedIn resume, Willie has also been a teacher of yoga and meditation which is a big part of how this book came to be. Professionally, he has also been fortunate enough to be paid as an artist (painting), a musician, and now is incredibly excited to add the title of author to the list.

www.ingramcontent.com/pod-product-compliance
Lightning Source LLC
LaVergne TN
LVHW011407080426
835511LV00005B/426